I **hope** you enjoy reading
"Falling in Love with Baseball"
as much as I did writing it

Chris "Mavo" Mavraedis

Falling in Love with Baseball

THE 1958 SAN FRANCISCO GIANTS

Falling in Love with Baseball

By Chris Mavraedis

Edited by Bob Sockolov

Forewords by Bruce Bochy and Marty Lurie

CHRONICLE BOOKS
SAN FRANCISCO

ISBN: 978-1-4521-6664-3

Manufactured in the United States of America.

Design by Jill Sockolov, www.JillSock.com

Photographs © San Francisco Giants Archive unless otherwise noted.
Photographs on pages 10 and 44 © Jill Sockolov.
Photographs on pages 5, 8, and 30 reprinted courtesy of Robert and Audrey Sockolov.
Photograph on pages 11, 15, and 24 reprinted courtesy of Chris Mavraedis.
Photograph on page 27 from iStock.com.

10 9 8 7 6 5 4 3 2 1

Chronicle Books LLC
680 Second Street
San Francisco, CA 94107

www.chroniclebooks.com/custom

Page 2: The 1958 San Francisco Giants *From left, front row:* **Batboys Boy McKercher and Frank Iverlish;** *first row:* **Felipe Alou, Willie Mays, Jim Davenport, Willie Kirkland, Coach Wes Westrum, Manager Bill Rigney, Coach Herman Franks, Coach Salty Parker, Ruben Gomez, Orlando Cepeda, Bill White;** *second row:* **Equipment Manager Eddie Logan, Don Johnson, Paul Giel, Nick Testa, Al Worthington, Jackie Brandy, Stu Miller, Danny O'Connell, Gordon Jones, Whitey Lockman, Daryl Spender, Trainer Bowman;** *third row:* **Ramon Monzant, Hank Sauer, Bob Schmidt, Bob Speake, Eddie Bressoud, John Antonelli, Ray Jablonksi, Valmy Thomas, Mike McCormick**

Robert Sockolov posing with the San Francisco Giants' 2010 World Series trophy

Editor's Note

A substantial portion of the profits from the sale of this book will be donated to The ALS Association Golden West Chapter to aid in the search for the prevention and cure for the debilitating effects of Lou Gehrig's Disease. Chris Mavraedis, the author of these memories and stories, has been a victim of ALS and has persevered through his illness with the help of his "love of baseball." It has sustained him and given him motivation in his fight to survive. To learn more about the fight against ALS, visit alsa.org.

Acknowledgments

Thanks to the San Francisco Giants: President and CEO Larry Baer, Mario Alioto, Nancy Donati, Shana Daum, and especially to Missy Mikulecky, Director of the San Francisco Giants Photo Archives.

Thanks to the following for their advice and support: Jay Sondheim, Rabbi Martin Weiner, Joelle Benioff, Anders Nancke-Krogh, Mark Devereaux, Kristin Woodruff, Dawn Boyer Comer, John Keker, Mike Strunsky, Tyler Peterson, Aaron Haesler, and Audrey Sockolov.

Thanks to the ALS Association Golden West Chapter for their research and endeavors to halt ALS.

This book is much improved due to the efforts of these Chronicle Books people: Catherine Huchting, Pamela Geismar, Laurel Leigh, and Beth Weber. Thanks!

Very special thanks to Robert "Bob" L. Sockolov, Jill Sockolov, and Elizabeth "Liz" Mavraedis.

A young Willie Mays playing
stickball in Harlem

Contents

Foreword by Bruce Bochy

Clockwise from top left: **Kim Bochy, Bruce Bochy, Elizabeth Mavraedis, and Chris Mavraedis**

I have been blessed to be involved with this great game of baseball my entire life. As I read through Chris Mavraedis's remembrances of *Falling in Love with Baseball*, so many great memories resurfaced for me. Memories such as the precious and wonderful times that I had with my father, either listening on the radio or going to a game together. All the friends whom I played with or against and how so many years later everyone can still vividly remember the details of those games. Attending my very first major league game as a ten-year-old with my dad to see the Senators play in Washington, D.C. You never forget that first look at the beauty and majesty of a major league baseball field! That was the moment I knew I wanted to be a major leaguer. Also, of course, on this amazing run, I am fortunate to have been a major league player as well as manager.

I know the wonderful stories in this book about Mays, McCovey, Marichal, and all the other great players will bring back many special memories for Giants fans everywhere. I feel blessed to be a part of this storied franchise, and when I read Chris's beautiful stories about growing up with the Giants that feeling resonated even more so.

What a delightful read! Chris's passion and love for the game exudes throughout. It lets us understand the correlation between this game and our life battles off the field. Chris's on-field attitude and deep passion has extended to his ALS fight. Thanks for sharing, Chris, and for triggering the memories of what made each of us fall in love with baseball!

Foreword by Marty Lurie

What separates baseball from all the other sports are the stories of the game. These stories that cover more than 150 years of baseball connect families, friends, coworkers, and strangers in the sweetest way.

Falling in Love with Baseball, a collection of the baseball remembrances of Chris Mavraedis, takes one back through the times of the San Francisco Giants, from their first season in Seals Stadium to Candlestick Park and finally to the best baseball park in America, AT&T Park. Along the journey, Chris connects us to the iconic names of Giants history with personal stories about the greats, such as Willie Mays, Juan Marichal, and so many others. But it's not just the names, it's the intimate details Chris relates about the players, his personal experiences seeing or listening to the games with his father, and the grace of baseball he fell in love with as a boy that touch my heart. Personally, I love bringing the stories of baseball to the fans through my pre- and post-game

Giants radio shows on KNBR 680. Chris is my most faithful listener, often commenting on the segments connecting Giants history within moments of the broadcast. Trust me, I double-check my facts, knowing Chris is listening to each word.

Chris suffers from ALS, the dreaded Lou Gehrig's Disease. He is the most courageous, remarkable person I have ever met in baseball. His love for baseball comes across marvelously. When I read Chris's e-mails after a show, I say to myself, "How in the world does Chris write with such perfect detail about these baseball memories?"

This collection of Chris's writings is a must-read for any baseball fan. "As one stares out the window waiting for winter to end and spring training to begin" (quote from the great Rogers Hornsby), pick up this book; it will warm your heart in a way you'll never forget.

You are a special man, Chris Mavraedis.

Preface

I know the precise moment I began falling in love with baseball. It was April 1958, and the newly minted San Francisco Giants were playing their second week in Seals Stadium. My father and grandfather held my hands as they led me up the ramp. When we emerged into the brilliant sunshine, I was flabbergasted by what my eyes beheld. It was love at first sight! Spread out before my six-year-old eyes was the impossibly vast expanse of the bright emerald green grass of Seals Stadium. I don't remember what team the Giants were playing. I do remember being enraptured by the distances the ball flew and how the graceful Giants' center fielder glided about the broad green expanse to catch the impossibly high-hit fly balls. His name was of course Willie Mays, the incomparable superstar, and he became my childhood idol that sunny, breezy, blue-sky afternoon.

Thus began my lifelong love affair with baseball. This book is a collection of short stories describing my memories of being a fan of the Giants as well as my own memories of playing our great game. Most of the stories originally took the form of e-mails that I sent to family and friends over the past decade. Fittingly, there are 24 stories in this book to honor my childhood idol and the best baseball player

of all time—Willie Mays. Baseball fans need no explanation of the significance of 24, the number Willie wore with such distinction and class for 22 stellar years.

I was born in San Francisco's Mission District at Mary's Help Hospital (now Seton Medical Center in Daly City), which stood directly across the street from the former Recreation Park, the ballpark that the San Francisco Seals played in for 27 years prior to Seals Stadium. So, right from birth I've had San Francisco baseball in my blood.

In 2009, I was diagnosed with ALS, or Lou Gehrig's Disease (even this terrible disease has a baseball connection). In my seven-year battle with this horrendous disease, I've slowly lost the ability to speak clearly. As the disease progressed, I took to writing as my primary way of communicating my thoughts. I've never thought of myself as a particularly good writer, but when I posted my stories on baseball blogs and sent them out to family and friends, I received an overwhelming number of positive reactions. This surprised me! KNBR 680's Marty Lurie, the excellent host of pre- and post-game for Giants broadcasts, even read some of my stories on the air. I was extremely flattered when the talented baseball writer, Andrew Baggarly, asked if

he could publish my story of the greatest pitchers' duel of the twentieth century on the CSN Bay Area website on the fiftieth anniversary of the duel in 2013. I'm referring, of course, to the classic sixteen-inning pitchers' duel between a young Juan Marichal and the ageless Warren Spahn at Candlestick Park in 1963. Although CSNBA recently removed that story, you can read an improved version of it in this book.

But the real reason you hold this book in your hands is due to my dear friend Robert Sockolov. Bob asked me for several years to gather together my stories for possible publication. Being flattered but thinking he was just being kind, I dragged my feet getting my stories and e-mails to him. Finally, when my lovely wife, Elizabeth, and I saw Bob and his beautiful wife, Audrey, at a rare in-person Giants game we attended last year, I began organizing my writing for Bob. Upon receiving the manuscript, he sprung into action! Within weeks Bob, Audrey, and their lovely granddaughter, Jill, produced a draft layout for this book. My wife and I were delighted with the initial mock-up. How Bob and Audrey did it so quickly belied their octogenarian ages!

I'm totally indebted to Bob and Audrey, who are minority owners of the San Francisco Giants, for the fact that *Falling in Love with Baseball* has been published. Thank you both! I don't think it's possible for me to ever repay you for your generosity and hard work on this project.

I'd also like to thank Jill Sockolov for her skill and hard work in designing this book along with photo and archive director Missy Mikulecky of the Giants. They both contributed a lot to this endeavor.

Thanks to my father and both my grandfathers for passing on the love of baseball to me at such a young, impressionable age. To my dear loving mother who drove me to years of practices and games, thanks, Mom! And kudos to the wonderful nurses who have helped keep me going these past seven years.

To all my fellow Giants fans in sections 122 and 123—you know who you are—thanks for all the great times we've shared. In the words of our beloved broadcaster, Mike Krukow, you're all Gamers and Gamer Babes!

A big tip of the cap to future Hall of Fame manager of the only three San Francisco Giants World Series championships, Bruce Bochy, for contributing the foreword to this book. Bruce and his gorgeous wife, Kim, are neighbors in our building. Thanks, Boch!

Thanks to Marty Lurie, KNBR 680's talented host, for contributing a second foreword. In many ways, this book wouldn't have been possible without Marty's encouragement by reading my writing on the air. Thanks, Marty!

Finally, to my beautiful wife of thirty years, Elizabeth. Without her love and care through this battle with the monster that ALS is, none of this would have been written. Thank you from the bottom of my heart, Babydoll!

—Chris Mavraedis
May 2017

From left, top: Chris Mavraedis, Elizabeth Mavraedis, Nancy Connell, Jack Connell; *bottom:* Michelle Ferrera, Joe Miller, Sherri Miller, Don O'Leary; at game three of the 2002 World Series

Number 24

Willie Mays celebrating his eightieth birthday on the field

Here's a birthday greetings e-mail I wrote to my baseball idol, Willie Mays, in celebration of his eightieth birthday. I really did not expect to get any response, as I am sure he was inundated with birthday wishes, given his fame as an American icon. Imagine my surprise when I got a personal message back from Willie!

May 6, 2011

Happy 80th birthday, Willie! I hope you celebrate this milestone day in good health with your friends and loved ones.

Due to my illness, unfortunately, I cannot attend the game tonight where they are going to honor you on this special day. But please believe me, I will be there in spirit wishing you all the best!

You may not remember me. I am the friend of Bob and Audrey Sockolov who has ALS or Lou Gehrig's Disease. Not only did you graciously sign your autobiography for me, you also thrilled and inspired me with a phone call last April to tell me to keep on fighting. That phone call was one of the most special things that have happened to me, Willie. I have used your inspirational call and words many times when my spirits get down and things get difficult with this terrible disease. I am sitting here, as I write this, looking at the autographed ball you gave me when I got to visit your suite a few years ago, thanks to my dear friends Bob and Audrey.

I have loved the Giants and have loved baseball since I was six years old, when I was taken to my first game at Seals Stadium in 1958, your first year in San Francisco. I remember being captivated by how green the grass was, and how gracefully a young man glided across the field in center field to catch fly balls that seemed so high to me. Willie, you must hear this many, many times, but believe me, I am not exaggerating one bit when I tell you that I have idolized you since those days. I collected all your baseball cards. I cut your picture out of magazines to put up on my bedroom wall. I followed your every move on the field whenever I could get out to Candlestick to watch you play. I copied your semi-underhand flip back into the infield. I copied to the best of my ability your stance in the batter's box when I played baseball. I even got bruises on my chest, not to mention a chewing out from my skipper for dropping a few, from foolishly trying to imitate your signature basket catch! I have literally lived and breathed Giants baseball all these years. I cried each time we were nosed out for the pennant in those frustrating years after 1962. And

I cried even as a nineteen-year-old when you were traded to the Mets in 1972.

So you can imagine how it touched me deeply to have my childhood idol, Willie Mays, call me to wish me well and inspire me to keep fighting. Well, Willie, thanks to you, I am still fighting! Your kindness and humanity to take the time to call me has meant a lot to me during the most difficult times lately. I fully intend to beat this disease in the end. When I do, I hope to be able to cook you up the delicious jambalaya dinner I promised you on the phone last year. It is not often that our childhood sports heroes, whom we idolize, turn out to be an even better human being than a sports hero!

So thank you from the bottom of my heart, Willie. I know you'll celebrate your 80th birthday in good health with many more to come. Willie, you are a Hall of Famer not only in Cooperstown, but most importantly, you are also a genuine Hall of Famer in *life*!

I am not exaggerating when I say I cried for a half an hour when I read the following response sent to Bob and Audrey by Willie's assistant, Rene.

. . . I have just read the letter to Willie and he has asked me to have it framed so that he can hang it on the wall in his home, where he has hung all the pictures of himself and Mae with various Presidents of the United States whom they have met over the years. He said, "That letter is as important to me as meeting the presidents." High praise from one who doesn't get overexcited about much of anything. Chris has really moved him.

Part of my disease severely heightens my emotions. But this message from Willie would've had me emotional regardless. Here's how I expressed it in an e-mail to family and friends:

Here I was trying to honor him on such a milestone birthday, and he honors me like this. I still am emotional thinking about it. What an honor to have this man as my childhood idol all these years. I did not know what a true superstar he was off the baseball field as well as on it. And as I write this, more than six years after Willie's inspirational phone call, I'm still fighting!

The Giants have retired Willie's number 24 and honored it with 24 palm trees in front of the ballpark along with the 24-foot-high brick wall in right field. I'm proud to dedicate the 24 stories that follow to my childhood hero.

1 *Falling in Love with Baseball*

Hall of Fame Dodgers pitcher Don Drysdale

Here's an e-mail I wrote to KNBR 680 host Marty Lurie. I first wrote to Marty when he became the pre- and post-game host for Giants games. It just so happens that this coincided with my losing my ability to speak clearly. Otherwise, I surely would have called in to his show.

You asked last time the Giants played the Dodgers for stories about how I got interested in the heated rivalry between the two teams. I sent you the story of how I refused to go with my father to the airport where he worked and the Dodgers parked their plane, for autographs when the Dodgers came to town—because they were *Dodgers*!

Well, here is another colorful story that cemented my love of baseball and the Giants vs. Dodgers rivalry. Maybe you can read this on the air sometime. Or maybe, when I beat this ALS and get my voice back, I can call in to tell it myself!

It was 1963, and the Giants were fighting the hated Dodgers for first place again after beating them in that dramatic three-game playoff the previous year. I was ten years old and literally lived and breathed baseball. My father, who along with my mother was raising six kids, could not take me out to many ball games back then. We lived in Fremont, and it was a long trip to Candlestick. But we got to the ballpark a few precious games a year anyway.

Well, this summer day the Giants were playing the Dodgers and it was Juan Marichal facing Don Drysdale at The Stick (Candlestick Park)! Marichal had thrown a no-hitter four days before and was my new pitching hero. My father was off work that day, and me being a typical ten-year-old, I worked on him all day long, begging for him to take me to the game that night. He kept saying no. And finally my mother told him to take me so I'd shut up.

My dad told me to get my coat and my glove. So we piled in the car and headed to the game kind of late. I had my glove and was excited that I'd get to see Juan Marichal pitch and my hero Willie Mays. It was the kind of excitement only a ten-year-old boy going to the game with his dad can feel.

When we arrived at The Stick, it was a sellout! At first, my dad thought we'd have to turn around and go home. I was crushed. The ticket teller noticed my ten-year-old anguish when my dad told me there were no tickets left, and he told my dad he could give us standing room tickets behind the outfield fences. My dad did not really want to stand up for three hours, but I got *really* excited, realizing I'd be closer to my hero Willie Mays if I was behind the outfield fences! I did not realize the center field area was not accessible behind the fences. So my dad, wonderful father that he was, bought the SRO tickets and we rushed in to get our spot. It was a typical windy, cold night game at The Stick especially where we were at in right field *before* they enclosed the stadium. It

was like a wind tunnel. But my good ol' dad hung in there with me. In my excitement, I didn't even notice it was cold.

We only could be in the right field area, almost straightaway right, actually. I raced right up to the fence and was in heaven being so close to the field. While we waited for the game to start, more and more fans crowded in behind us. The pitching match-up was drawing fans out of the woodwork for this one.

As they announced the starting lineups, I was devastated not to hear Willie Mays's name announced by Jeff Carter, the Giants PA announcer back then. Willie was sitting out this game! I seem to remember Willie had some kind of exhaustion problem about this time, but I could be wrong. He did not miss Giants vs. Dodgers very often. Probably just as well, as Drysdale always tried to nail Willie whenever he faced him. He never actually hit Willie, but he sent him sprawling in the dirt *every* time they faced each other, at least once a game.

Well, the game starts and in the first inning Willie McCovey, who absolutely *owned* Drysdale his whole career, hit a majestic, towering two-run home run way over my head. It was a typical Willie McCovey moon shot! I was amazed at how high and far that ball went, seeing it from ground level and being only ten. The batter's box looked like it was on another planet to my ten-year-old eyes. The ball landed halfway back in the SRO crowd gathered behind the right field fence. As the ball sailed over the fence, I found myself face-to-face with the Dodgers' right fielder, Ron Fairly, and all the fans were letting him have an earful you can be sure.

Later in the game, Willie Davis for the Dodgers tied the game on his own two-run homer to right again. This time I was fairly close to where the ball came down, but again no luck as there was no room to move back with the crowd pressing up behind us. But this time, I came face-to-face with Harvey Kuenn, the Giants' right fielder. He ran all the way to the fence and as the ball sailed just over my head on the other side, he says, "Aw, shit!" and he unloads a big wad of tobacco juice right on my shoe. He looks at me and says, "Sorry, kid!" and runs back

to his position. I was in shock that a big leaguer spit tobacco right on my shoe! But my grandfather chewed tobacco so it did not gross me out too bad. My dad just laughed and asked if I was having fun. I said I was until the Dodgers tied the game. Now Juan could not get a shutout!

The Giants went ahead soon after that, and they chased Drysdale. Meanwhile, I was getting into the spirit of dogging Fairly with some verbal abuse, nothing nasty, just calling him a bum, things like that. Well, the Giants had a nice lead and in the top of the eighth who should hit a home run off Marichal—Ron Fairly! And this time I almost caught it. But the people behind us pushed me right up against the fence, as it was close this time. As Harvey Kuenn got to the fence and saw the ball sail over, he saw me smashed up against the fence and said to me, "You all right, kid?" With my eyes as big as saucers, I said, "Yes, but I almost had that one!" And he winked at me with that big chaw in his mouth, but this time he didn't spit on me at least.

Bottom of the inning now and Ron Fairly is giving *us* guff as he is warming up. He is crowing about his home run and laughing at us. Well, wouldn't you know it, Chuck Hiller, the Giants' little second baseman, who hardly ever hit home runs (except grand slams in the World Series in Yankee Stadium!), hits a rare home run, again to right field. Again, I could not quite get to it but tried mightily to catch that ball! I was so upset. Four home runs

to my area, and I could not catch a single one even though I had brought my glove. And to add insult to injury, Ron Fairly laughed at me before he started back to his position. Seems he had identified me as one of the hecklers earlier.

But now is the best part. The Giants were warming up before the ninth inning. I noticed Harvey Kuenn running back to the fence. I thought he must have dropped something back there. I didn't even notice he had a ball in his glove. He comes right up to me at the fence and says, "Here, kid!" and drops a baseball just over the fence, right into my glove. I could not believe it at first! A major leaguer just gave me a big league ball. Finally, it dawned on me how I had just won the ten-year-old baseball lottery. I began jumping up and down and screaming. Harvey Kuenn turned around and just smiled at me. My dad said thanks to him, and I had my first major league baseball, not to mention a nasty tobacco stain on my Keds! I couldn't wait to get home and show all my Little League teammates what I had. As Kruk likes to say, "Betcha don't have one of *theese*!"

The Giants won that game 8–3, and I was a happy kid all the way home. I never got a chance to thank Harvey Kuenn for that baseball. But he always was my favorite player after that, outside of Willie Mays of course, even when he got traded to the Cubs a few years later. And you can bet I was pulling for Harvey's Wallbangers in the 1982 World Series! It was a sad day when I learned Harvey had passed away at way too young an age. It felt like an important part of my childhood had also died with him.

I did get to tell this story to Ron Fairly back when he was a Giants announcer in the 1980s. He said he *did* remember that particular game but not the snot-nosed ten-year-old who was heckling him behind the right field fence that day!

So that game kind of sums up how I fell in love with not just baseball but also with the Giants vs. Dodgers rivalry. And now thanks to the magic of the Internet and baseball-reference.com, I now know the exact date of that momentous game in my baseball childhood: June 19, 1963. I never did wash that tobacco stain off my shoe . . . but I outgrew that pair of shoes in months!

•••

A sellout at The Stick

2
First Time Donning the Tools of Ignorance

A few years ago, I was researching my family history online late one night. Because Mavraedis is so frequently misspelled, I put in some alternate spellings. I was surprised and totally delighted when up popped an old newspaper that had a picture of me catching my second game—in 1965 when I was twelve years old! At the time, I had no idea this photo had appeared in the local newspaper. How would I? I was twelve! As far as I know, it is the earliest photo of me playing baseball.

It was during a tournament game where my Little League team was sadly eliminated. Our team, the R & R Construction Yankees, had really torn up the inaugural season of the Fremont American Little League that summer. We went something like 15–1, only losing to the last-place team towards the end of the season. Not to brag, but we were so dominant that for the All-Star Game that year our team played the All-Stars from the rest of the league! I got to pitch to start the game, and I got blasted. In the end, our proud championship team got stomped 13–5. But at least we were clearly the dominant team of the league that year.

I batted cleanup on that team and played outfield with a bit of pitching too. But when it was time for us to play in the tournament in August, our catcher had to leave for his family vacation. Our skipper,

Mr. Lamont, a great youth baseball coach, decided I would catch my first game ever—in the tournament! I practiced extremely diligently and, swallowing hard, we won the first-round tournament game.

The photo I found shows me in my second game, "in the squat," as Giants announcer Mike Krukow so colorfully puts it. In this game, we ran into a monster on the mound. His name was Fisher, he looked about six-foot-two! He appeared much older that twelve and was throwing absolute smoke from that mound, which is a mere forty-four feet away in Little League. Our proud mini Fremont version of the Bronx Bombers got shut out 2–0 by The Monster.

We got two base runners on with two outs in the last inning, and I came up with a chance to win the game. I pictured another "walk-off home run" as I'd hit off my best friend a few months before. But

Chris Mavraedis catching his second game on August 7, 1965

miracles don't usually happen twice. I got a good, healthy home run swing at a curveball The Monster threw, but I popped out to end the game, tournament, and season for our brave little team. Our tournament was *over*! It was a shame because we truly had a great team that everyone thought would go far in the tournament. We all learned the old baseball maxim the hard way—good pitching beats good hitting!

So, that's the backstory of the old photo that appeared on August 8, 1965, in our local newspaper.. It was just over fifty years ago! This was before I learned from Johnny Bench and hard experience to tuck my throwing hand behind my back. And they didn't butcher Mavraedis in the photo caption too badly!

•••

Buster Posey geared
up for the game

3 *A Little League Drama from Fifty Years Ago*

Marshall Mavraedis, the author's nephew

While watching the 2015 Little League World Series, I was reminded of my sweetest baseball memory. It happened fifty years ago, during the best year I ever had playing baseball. So in honor of the Little League World Series, I sent family and friends this e-mail telling about my own Little League drama from 1965.

It was 1965, I was twelve years old, and Fremont, California, got its first Little Leagues. Because Fremont was so big areawise, two leagues were formed: the Fremont American and Fremont National Little Leagues. After tryouts, I was selected by the R & R Construction Yankees of the American League.

Our team was really dominating that inaugural year! We had a great youth baseball coach who had played some professional baseball. Mr. Lamont not only had a great eye for potential, he taught us all more baseball than most of us would ever dream to learn!

We won the first thirteen games and left the second-place Red Sox in the dust by five games or so. When our league held its first All-Star Game, it was decided our Yankees team would play the other All-

Stars from the rest of the teams! We got clobbered, but it showed what a good team we had.

Now that I've set the scene, here's the main story. We were playing the second-place Red Sox towards the end of the season, and were in danger of losing our first game. They held a two-run lead going into the bottom of the last inning. The first batter was retired. Our leadoff hitter, a fine center fielder named Billy Toth, got a hit. The second-place hitter, our coach's son, Ray Lamont, bounced a hit up the middle. The third-place batter was our hard-hitting All-Star shortstop, Dave Beebe, who was also a power hitter. With two on, Beebe could win it with a home run. He popped out, and it was my turn. We were down to our last out. But I was confident because I usually hit this pitcher very well. I already had two line drive hits off him in this game. Then something unexpected happened.

The Red Sox manager went to the mound and motioned one of my best friends, Jerry, in to face me! This was unexpected because Jerry hadn't pitched before, that I knew of anyway. He definitely hadn't faced us on the mound before. I remember first being surprised, but my next reaction was a feeling of great confidence.

Why did I feel so supremely confident? Because I'd played sandlot ball with Jerry for years! We used to get together as many kids from the neighborhood

as possible and literally play all day long with only a break for lunch and dinner. This was decades before video games, and we played sports year round. Summer was our prime time, obviously, and baseball was *the* game. I'd gotten my lifelong nickname of "Mavo" during one of those summer days playing baseball in the park. One of the kids got tired of trying to pronounce Mavraedis and began calling me Mavo, as my close friends do to this day. So I had probably played hundreds if not a thousand hours of baseball with my buddy Jerry during those long, warm summer days.

As Jerry trotted in from center field and got to the mound we made eye contact. I just smiled, but Jerry was serious! He was obviously nervous, and his Red Sox desperately wanted to take down the mighty undefeated Yankees! To me this was a psychological ploy by their manager to psych me out. He knew I had the power to win the game as I'd already had two hits off the first pitcher, and I was leading the league in home runs.

As Jerry started his warm-up tosses, I felt a tap on my shoulder. It was our skipper, Mr. Lamont. He asked me if I knew Jerry and had played ball with him. Smiling broadly, I blurted out, "Mr. Lamont, I've played tons of ball with Jerry and he cannot surprise me!" This pleased Mr. Lamont, and he said, "Great! Take some deep breaths, relax . . . wait for a

good pitch . . . and win this thing, Chris! You can do it!" Funny how all this is etched in my memory even after half a century has passed.

I stepped into the batter's box and clearly saw fear in Jerry's eyes, as he got ready to face me. He took his stretch and let go his first pitch. It was right down the heart of the plate, a "cookie" in baseball jargon. I swung hard and as soon as the ball made contact with my bat, I knew it was gone!

There's nothing like the feel of a hardball that hits the sweet spot on a wooden bat. It's an exquisite sensation, and the batter just knows he got all of it. The kids use aluminum bats all the way until they turn professional now. I feel sorry for the kids nowadays who never feel that sensational feeling of a baseball hitting the sweet spot on a wooden bat.

A split second after the ball left my bat with a sharp crack, it headed for the fence in straightaway center field. I vividly remember Billy, our little leadoff hitter, dancing and leaping for joy off second base. Being a center fielder, he knew where the ball was heading! The center fielder for the Red Sox took a few steps back towards the fence and then gave up. It sailed over the center field fence by a large distance. It was the longest home run I'd ever hit in Little League, or any baseball at that time!

I headed for first as all the Red Sox players slumped their shoulders and trudged off the field.

Jerry, head down, just walked off the mound after seeing the ball land. We'd won in the most dramatic way possible. I rounded the bases and met all my teammates at the plate. Mr. Lamont was there to meet me too, along with the other coaches. It was definitely a moment that no twelve-year-old kid would ever forget and I certainly have not, even after half a century.

The obligatory pizza and ice cream never tasted so good as that afternoon for my teammates and me. The following day, my dear mother woke me up by laying the sports section of the local paper on my face. She said, "You're famous! You made the paper!" I rubbed my eyes and saw the article headline in bold letters: "Marvadis Wins It for Undefeated Yanks!" They butchered my last name, but I was used to that by now. The article went on to recap the game, culminating in my dramatic home run to win it. The term "walk-off" wasn't coined yet. It was simply a game-winning home run then. Dennis Eckersley, a Hall of Fame pitcher also from Fremont, coined that colorful term over twenty years later. Somehow, I've lost that newspaper article over the years. I always thought I'd get the time to go to the Fremont library to look it up. But I never got the chance.

The story could've ended there, but there's another neat twist. Exactly twenty years later, in the summer of 1985, I'd recently started a new consulting assignment in Oakland. I was driving by Lake Merritt on Lakeshore Boulevard when an old beat-up car behind me started honking and blinking his lights. The driver looked rather shabbily dressed and was motioning me to pull over. I was not about to pull over for obvious reasons. I sped up, and the car behind me darted alongside me. The driver had the window down and was motioning for me to pull over. He started yelling, "Mavo, pull over!" I realized my personalized license plates were MAVO I. So I sped up more. Then the shady, suspicious driver yelled, "Mavo, pull over. It's Jerry!" I pulled over!

It turned out my old friend Jerry, with whom I'd lost contact years before, was an undercover narcotics officer for the Oakland police. That explained his shabby clothes and car. It was also why I didn't recognize him. We reminisced a bit, and I deliberately avoided bringing up that walk-off home run I'd hit off him twenty years before.

But as we were wrapping up our conversation, after agreeing to meet for lunch outside Oakland, he brought it up. He said, "I still remember that painful home run you hit off me twenty years ago, you . . ." He added an expletive that I won't repeat here. I smiled and said, "Still my most memorable moment in baseball!" He shot back, "I should've thrown you some chin music"—baseball jargon for throwing at a batter's chin. I replied, "If you'd done that, I'd have had to charge the mound!" We both chuckled and got in our cars to drive off.

I am currently fighting ALS, also known as Lou Gehrig's Disease. Given my love of baseball, it is ironic that Gehrig was one of the most famous baseball players ever and I have this disease named for him. I have more time to reminisce now, even though I cannot talk now. Thank goodness I can still write, albeit with some difficulty. Some childhood memories are forever vividly etched into our memory, even fifty-year-old memories! Every time I watch a Little League game or a walk-off home run, my mind takes me back to that warm summer day in Fremont in 1965 . . . and I smile.

•••

4
A Knuckleball Memory . . .
and a Few Baseball Lessons

Here is an e-mail I sent to friends, family, and a baseball blog in late July 2014, when Brandon Belt and Héctor Sánchez were on the disabled list with concussions.

I am very concerned about both Brandon Belt and Héctor Sánchez. Concussions are serious business. Given what happened to former Giants catcher Mike Matheny, and how his career was cut abruptly short by a concussion, I am sure the Giants are sufficiently worried! First, I'd ban those hockey-style masks. I think they lead to more concussions, maybe by having the sound trauma in the ear when the ball hits that mask. Go back to the old heavy steel masks that I wore forty years ago when I caught.

I had a couple of experiences with concussions from a motorcycle accident, a fight (where I took a nasty sucker punch!), football, and baseball. There are those who feel repeated concussions may have led to me contracting Lou Gehrig's Disease. I don't know about that. But I was reminded of a story I wrote last year about a bad concussion I got while playing semi-pro baseball years ago. Here's that story from last year:

I was watching the series *The Next Knuckler* on MLB Network and in one episode, Jarrod Saltalamacchia, the Red Sox catcher, was walking by one of the young catchers taking knuckleballs from the contestants. Salty noticed the young catcher was not wearing a mask. He said, "Brave, son, to not wear a mask catching a knuckler!" When he said that I chuckled and a memory flooded back to me from forty years ago, when I had a very intimate encounter with how stupid it is to catch a knuckleball pitcher without a mask on, even during warm-ups!

Hall of Fame knuckleballer James Hoyt
Wilhelm of the New York Giants

Out of high school, I had a young family and could not immediately go to college. I wanted to keep playing baseball, so I began playing on a semi-pro team in Fremont. I was a catcher and played one season before finally giving up the dream of playing pro baseball and going to college.

We had an older pitcher in his late thirties, named Don Curly, who was a knuckleballer. He had played some pro ball and did not ever make it. Man, the first time I caught him I got a real workout. I learned that what Bob Uecker, a.k.a. Mr. Baseball, said about catching a knuckleball was so true: "The best way to catch a knuckleball is to wait for it to stop rolling and pick it up!"

The only reason Don was not ever in the majors was that one out of three of his knucklers did nothing and was a fat BP pitch that was usually hit a *long* way. But when he floated a good one up there, I swear it danced as well as any Hoyt Wilhelm "butterfly" ever did! Of course, back then I did not even have one of the newer big flexible catcher's mitts to try and wrestle one of his good "buterflies" down.

Early during my first year with the team, Don was not getting many of his knucklers to dance much and was getting bombed. We were preparing to play a local team, and Don was scheduled to pitch. I began to warm him up, without a mask, and he said I should put one on. I chuckled and said he wished he had a good enough knuckler to make me wear a mask! He shrugged and said, "It's your pretty face!"

As I warmed him up, an old teammate of mine who was on the opposing team noticed me and came over to chat with me. As we chatted and joked around,

Don floated a real beauty up there. As it fluttered closer, I lost sight of it as it dipped below my mitt. As I moved the mitt down to pick up sight of it, I waited for it to hit the glove. I never did see it again until SUDDENLY it was there! Coming over the top of my mitt! I tried to react, but it was way too late. It hit me square in the nose. Knocked me on my back, and the lights went out.

When I came to, all my teammates were around me and a spectator who was a doctor was holding my nose. He said, "How you doing, Chris? Don't move, as I think you've broken your nose and it is bleeding profusely!" He kept pressure on it to stop the bleeding and recommended I be taken to the hospital. I shook my head and, being a stupid nineteen-year-old, struggled to my feet. "I'll be all right with a few minutes." My teammates, none of whom wanted to catch that warm day, all cheered and helped me stagger to the bench.

I noticed a slight headache, and my nose was partially blocking my vision as it swelled up. The doctor showed up with an ice bag to keep the swelling down. After a few more minutes, I announced I was good and went to get on my gear, including a mask this time!

Did I make it through the game? I *did* somehow! It was a hot day, and while I had a headache, I gutted it out to catch all nine innings. I had to call time-out about five times when my nose started bleeding again. My vision remained partially blocked from the nose swelling, and I was a bit disoriented throughout the game. But I sucked it up and gutted it out—that's what was done in those days. It's like

Matheny getting hit in the mouth while batting and still toughing it out. Baseball is a macho game, and catchers are supposed to be the toughest of all.

I felt the effects in my at bats, as I struck out three times and popped out once . . . that never happened to me as the cleanup hitter. The final insult was that Don, the old knuckleballer, never threw another knuckler like the one that broke my nose again all game! He got torched and was gone in the third inning. We lost the game horribly, something like 11–2.

But it was the after-effects that cause me to be concerned for both Belt and Sánchez. We only had a month left to play. I had lingering effects from the concussion not only when playing ball, as I slumped badly, but also whenever I got my heart rate elevated with exercise. It was a good six months before I was normal again. And remember, I was nineteen with the recuperative powers of youth.

So yes, two important lessons learned:

1. The best way to catch a knuckleball is to follow Mr. Baseball's advice and wait for it to stop rolling, then pick it up!

2. *Never . . . ever . . .* warm up even an aging knuckleball pitcher without a mask! Preferably, one of those old-fashioned heavy steel ones I used in the distant past!

●●●

5

Meltdown on the Mound

Here is a story written for this book, recalling my second year of Fremont Babe Ruth baseball, when I was fourteen years old. Some names have been changed to preserve individual privacy.

It was summer of 1967, and we didn't have a very good team. We finished second to last that year. Our manager was a hotheaded curmudgeon I'll call Luis Silva. Nobody on the team liked playing for him, outside of his son, whom he favored at every opportunity.

I normally caught and pitched on that team. But I'd played way too much late-night Wiffle ball that spring. We used to play baseball after school for hours. We broke for dinner, of course—we were growing teenage boys and we ate everything in sight. After dinner, my brother or a good friend of mine and I would get under the streetlights and play Wiffle ball. The batter would stand on the sidewalk directly under the streetlight for the best light. The pitcher would stand on the other side of the street.

We would take turns firing that Wiffle ball and make it do amazing things. It would rise, drop, or curve crazily, depending on how we held the half with holes. This did wonders for our hitting breaking balls. But it totally shot our arms because we would

play for hours. God knows how many pitches we fired with that feather-light Wiffle ball.

As a consequence, when we started the season that year, my arm was killing me. I usually had a great arm, whether throwing from the crouch behind the plate or on the mound. Of course as a fourteen-year-old kid, I never equated the Wiffle ball marathons under the lights with my sore wing until years later.

After a few games behind the plate and pitching, my arm wasn't improving. Runners were stealing me blind when I was catching, and I was getting bombed when I pitched. Luis Silva, the manager, wanted to keep my bat in the lineup. Like Buster Posey, I batted cleanup. Because of those same Wiffle ball marathons that had hurt my arm, I was tearing the cover off the ball.

Mr. Silva moved me to first base until my arm hopefully healed. After a month, my arm still wasn't coming around. Every practice and before games I'd try to throw from home plate to second to see how the arm felt. I'd be pissed off and disappointed each

time I threw because it killed me! I didn't enjoy playing first base. I wanted to catch and pitch.

That summer my father was on an extended work assignment for American Airlines in Denmark. The rest of the family was scheduled to join him in late June, right in the middle of baseball season. I pleaded with my mother to let me stay home with a friend's family so I could finish the season. Back then, I literally lived and breathed baseball. My mother refused and said I'd enjoy the trip. She wanted me to have the experience of traveling to another country. She wasn't budging on this one; I was going to Denmark. Looking back almost fifty years, my mother was right, of course. Don't you hate it when, looking back, you now understand where your parents were coming from?

A week before I was reluctantly leaving for Denmark, we were getting shelled by the first-place team. It got to 8–2 with the bases loaded . . . for them. It was the fourth inning with only one out. Mr. Silva called time and went to the mound. I trotted over from first to the mound. Silva said, "Mavo, you're in there!" When I started to protest that my arm was still sore, he half yelled at me, "Enough excuses! You're in there! Get us out of this inning, and you'll be back at first next inning." Silva was a terrible loser, and we lost a lot that season. I thought, what the hell? Maybe he's right, and so I took the ball from him. I only needed two measly outs.

I thought my arm was all right, as I warmed up. But my motion and timing was all screwed up because I hadn't thrown off a mound for months. And this was the taller fifteen-inch-high mound back then. Baseball didn't lower it to ten inches high until two years later. It really wasn't fair to throw me out there on the mound with a sore arm and no practice. But that's what a hothead Mr. Silva was. He lost all judgment and his temper the further behind we fell, which we did a lot that season.

I wish this story had a happy, heroic ending. But the title of this story probably gave the ending away. There would be no happy ending this day. What happened next brings a big smile to my lips even now though.

With the adrenaline coursing through me, my arm felt fine the first two pitches. But they were nowhere near the plate. I walked the first batter to force in a run. 9–2! Mr. Silva, ever the great sportsman, yelled, "Christ!" and slammed his cap down.

Next batter hit one that whistled past my ear into center field—two more runs. 11–2! Mr. Silva almost swallowed his cigarette. My buddy Mike, who was catching, came out to give me a pep talk. No good—long double, two more runs. 13–2!! My arm was screaming by now. The harder I tried to throw, the further they hit it.

The next batter was their cleanup hitter, whom I'd played ball against for years. He had always owned me. Silva yelled, "C'mon, Chris! Strike this kid out!" I slowed it down and tried to shake some life into my barking arm. I tried to keep the pitch low and away from him. Nada, I grooved it right down Broadway—long home run to left. Two more runs. 15–2!!! I turned to watch how far the ball sailed over the fence. It impressed me even in my rage and embarrassment.

By the time I turned back to the plate to get another ball from the umpire, Mr. Silva was storming towards the mound, mumbling profanities, and his face was purple. I knew this wasn't gonna be a pep talk and a pat on the butt. But what happened still fries my ass.

As he approached the mound Silva was yelling, "Jesus Christ! My grandmother could pitch better! In fact, my son can pitch better!" His son Donnie was the littlest guy on the team and had never pitched. "Donnie, you're going to pitch," Silva spat out. "Give me the ball!" he said to me, holding his hand out.

I snapped! It takes a lot to get me mad. But it is not pretty when I do boil over. I looked at Mr. Silva bug-eyed as he tried to grab the ball from my hand. I screamed, "You want the ball? You want the *bleeping* ball? Here's your *bleeping* ball!" With that, I heaved the ball across the street adjacent to the field. "FETCH!" was my final word. I heard some muffled giggles from my teammates as Mr. Silva just stood there in shock.

I stormed off the field, listening to Mr. Silva's tirade. I walked the one mile home . . . in my cleats. Would I have done this if I hadn't been leaving for Denmark in a week? Hell, yes, I would have! Mr.

Silva was way out of line. No young ballplayer should be treated like that.

A few months later, Mr. Silva tried to get me barred from the league the following season. But other coaches and parents had protested his behavior. A few players quit the team after I did. It turned out that he was the one who almost got barred from the league. Somehow, he avoided being barred and managed a different team the following season.

I was declared a "free agent," and teams drew numbers out of a hat for the right to have me on their team. I wound up with a team managed by a great man I'd known since Little League. I was ecstatic, and I looked forward to the next baseball season and my revenge against Mr. Silva's new team. But that's a whole other story, and it will have to wait for a retelling (see "Sequel to Meltdown on the Mound" on page 74).

Denmark was a great experience that I'm very glad I didn't miss. Sure, I missed baseball terribly. It was very difficult to get the scores of MLB games in those pre-Internet Dark Ages. Oftentimes I would go into work with my father at the airport to act as his "gopher." When I had the chance, I'd rummage through the airplanes before they were cleaned in hopes of finding a *Sporting News* or any US newspaper to get my baseball fix!

That summer the American League had a pennant race for the ages. As it turned out, it was the final, epic pure pennant race before divisional play

was introduced in 1969. It was excruciating for me to have a baseball blackout all summer. But somehow, I survived, and we got home just in time for game one of the World Series between the Red Sox and the Cardinals. At least the damn Dodgers weren't in their third straight World Series! The great Sandy Koufax had retired before that season.

One final thought: My "fetch" heave that day in 1967 was the best damned pitch I threw all year.

•••

6 Fiftieth Anniversary of the First San Francisco Giants' No-Hitter

Fondly known as the Dominican Dandy, Juan Marichal threw the first no-hitter in San Francisco Giants history on June 15, 1963, against the Houston Colt .45s. This is an e-mail written in 2013, on the fiftieth anniversary of that historic game.

1963 was the year we all knew the Dominican Dandy was going to be a true dominant star pitcher!

The Cy Young Award was established in 1956 to honor the best pitcher in MLB that season. It was named for the pitcher who won the most games in MLB history. While now they award a Cy Young Award for each league, the first eleven years there was only one award given for MLB.

In 1963 Juan had a year which normally would have given him the Cy Young Award, after going 25–8! But as usual, Sandy Koufax went crazy in L.A. that year. Juan did not get a single vote for the Cy Young, and with good reason. Koufax had his first truly dominant season that year, going 25–5, ERA of 1.88, and striking out over three hundred for the first time! No wonder he won the Cy Young Award unanimously with all twenty votes! Sandy also captured the Most Valuable Player Award in the NL for his outstanding 1963 season.

This happened year after year to Juan. He'd have an outstanding season, but somebody, usually Koufax or Gibson, would have a year for the ages and Juan would get shut out in the Cy Young voting! Four times Juan had truly outstanding seasons, but Koufax or Gibson won the Cy Young Award unanimously! Sandy won the Cy Young three times unanimously, and in 1968 Bob Gibson did it also with maybe the best pitching performance in history.

Talk about bad timing for a pitcher. Do you realize that Juan did not get a single Cy Young vote until 1971, his last effective year? I had high hopes in 1967, when they split the Cy Young by league and gave two awards. But Juan had his first injury that year and lefty Mike McCormick won the first Cy Young Award for the Giants. Then in 1969, I had hopes again for Juan, but Tom "Terrific" Seaver beat him out even though Juan had the best ERA and won 20. Juan did not get a single vote even in 1969!

A funny story about the day Juan Marichal threw his no-hitter . . . It was a Saturday game, and I was pitching that day for my Little League team. I was pitching pretty well and we were winning late, when suddenly, as I was about to throw a pitch, the crowd went bonkers, cheering wildly! I was caught off guard and threw the pitch to the backstop. I found out at the end of the inning that they were all listening to Juan's final inning at The Stick. LOL! So it was not *my* outstanding pitching they were cheering, it was Juan's!

The Giants won that day 1–0 as the Colt .45s' pitcher, a journeyman named Dick Drott, threw a three-hitter and only gave up a lone run in the bottom of the eighth. The only regret I had was not being able to listen to the end of the game. My father had it on the car radio when he was driving me to my game. But neither one of us knew Juan had not allowed a hit yet when my game started.

So I hope you remember the *best* pitcher in San Francisco Giants history. Sorry Tim Lincecum, you won two Cy Young's but you did not have Koufax, Gibson, and Seaver keeping you from the hardware!

•••

This story began as an e-mail sent to family, friends and posted on a baseball blog a few days before the fiftieth anniversary of the 1963 Giants vs. Braves game. Journalist Andrew Baggarly posted the original version of this story on the CSNBA website.

This Tuesday, July 2, 2013, is the 50th anniversary of a remarkable historic baseball game played in our own Candlestick Park. It was perhaps the best pitchers' duel of the live ball era (which dates from 1920). I am, of course, referring to the magnificent duel between Warren Spahn of the Milwaukee Braves and Juan Marichal of the San Francisco Giants. Both hurlers in this pitching duel for the ages are Hall of Fame members. Undoubtedly, they both rank among the best pitchers in baseball history.

Let's set the stage for this drama. The Giants were in their sixth season in San Francisco. They were defending NL champions and, had a line drive been a foot or two higher the previous October, would have been the defending World Champions. But that is a story for another day. The Giants were loaded with stars, especially sluggers, destined for the Hall of Fame. They were in the midst of a run of excellence that would see them win the most games in the NL for the decade of the 1960s.

The Milwaukee Braves were in their eleventh season in that city after they had fled Boston in 1953. They were two-time NL champions in the late '50s and

Juan Marichal and Warren Spahn after their sixteen-inning classic duel still were a force to be reckoned with in the NL that season of 1963. The Braves also had multiple stars destined for enshrinement in Cooperstown.

Both teams were some of the first, along with the Dodgers, to recognize and sign the deep talent pool of African American and Latin American players. As a result, they were perennial contenders for the pennant.

The two co–home run leaders for that season of 1963, Henry "Hank" Aaron and Willie "Stretch" McCovey, played in the game, both future Hall of Famers. Strangely, they tied with 44 home runs that season, the same as both their uniform numbers! Numerologists would have a field day with that one! Both of them hailed from Mobile, Alabama. In fact, Willie McCovey chose 44 as his uniform number when he broke in 1959 because it was his idol's . . . Henry Aaron's number! Of course, Henry Aaron would go on to break the most hallowed of all baseball records: Babe Ruth's career home run total of 714 and wind up his career as the all-time home run leader with 755.

This game also featured the other two top home run leaders for the NL that year. That meant all four of the NL home run leaders played that night. The NL home run leaders were, in order: Aaron 44, McCovey 44, Mays 38, Cepeda 34. So the game did not lack for power hitters! The power-laden Giants, even in windy Candlestick, would lead the league in home runs that season by a large margin: 197 over the Braves at 139.

But the key actors in this drama that would make Shakespeare proud were Marichal, Spahn, and, in my opinion, the best ballplayer to ever lace up his spikes . . . Willie Mays!

The contrast between the two pitchers could not have been more stark. Marichal was a hard-throwing right-hander of twenty-five who was having his first great season. Spahn was a left-hander of forty-two who was having the last great year of a stellar career. Both would win over 20 that year (Marichal 25 and Spahn 23) Yet both would not get a single vote for the Cy Young Award because a lefty named Sandy Koufax was beginning the greatest four-year run of pitching dominance in baseball history.

When the Tuesday evening game started at eight p.m., Marichal came in with a record of 12–3 and Spahn was 11–3. Both pitchers featured a high leg kick in their delivery, but the similarity of these two pitchers ended there.

Spahn was the crafty old veteran left-hander who got by on wile and experience. Spahnie, as he was known, already had well over three hundred victories. And that was including him missing three whole years of his prime while fighting in World War Two. Spahn had thrown a three-hit shutout just four days prior at Dodger Stadium.

Marichal was a fire-balling right-hander with great control who had thrown a no-hitter only seventeen days prior. Marichal was, just that season, becoming the undisputed ace of the Giants staff.

Spahn had no-hit these same powerful Giants two years before on April 28, 1961, five days after his fortieth birthday. Incidentally, two days after that no-hitter tossed by Spahn, Willie Mays tied the single game home run record by clouting four in a game.

On a personal note, I quit a heated neighborhood ball game in the park to go home and listen to this game on KSFO. I knew it was going to be a good match-up, but I could not have imagined how historic it would be. So after a quick dinner, I hustled out to the living room where my dad had his large console stereo set, wood and all. It was about five feet long. I tuned in to Russ Hodges and Lon Simmons and lay down on the carpet to have the two large speakers by my head. Of course, I had my trusty glove with me and tossed an old beat-up ball in the air as I listened. I was ten years old and already totally in love with baseball.

The game started as you'd expect; both pitchers looked in good form. There was no real scoring threat through the first three innings. Marichal had only given up a single in the first. Spahn had also only given up a single to Orlando Cepeda in the second. Even though Cepeda stole second, he died at third when José Pagán, the Giants' shortstop, fouled out.

In the fourth, the Braves mounted a rally off Marichal. After Marichal retired the two Braves' Hall of Fame sluggers, Hank Aaron and Eddie Mathews, he walked Norm Larker, the Braves' first baseman. Mack Jones, a slugger in his own right, hit a single to get on and Larker moved to second. Here, one of our trio of heroes made his first big contribution. Del Crandall, the Braves' fine catcher, lined a single to center. Willie Mays, the finest center fielder in history, fielded it and gunned down Larker at the plate as he tried to score from second! The score was still 0–0 headed to the bottom of the fourth.

Eddie Mathews left the game starting the bottom of the fourth due to injury. Denis Menke, a fine young utility player, replaced him in the cleanup spot. The Giants managed a single by McCovey in the bottom of that inning, but Spahn did not let him get past first as he set down the Giants, 0–0 going to the fifth.

The next scare came in the top of the seventh. The Braves' Crandall led off with a single. The Braves had stolen two bases in the two previous innings, but Marichal pitched out of it. Now, with Crandall on first and the bottom of the Braves order up, he tried to steal second, also. Ed Bailey gunned him down for out number one. Then with two down, Warren Spahn,

who was a fine hitting pitcher who hit 35 home runs in his career, doubled. He was stranded at second, though, when Marichal got Lee Maye on a grounder to first. It was still 0–0 going to the bottom of the seventh, and both pitchers still looked strong. In this era of no pitch counts, neither manager remotely considered taking out his ace!

The Giants scratched out two singles against Spahn in the bottom of the seventh. But they came with two outs and both runners were stranded when pinch hitter Jimmy Davenport flew out to end the inning. Still 0–0, and the tension was building heading to the eighth inning.

It was about this time I started realizing how lucky I was that it was a summer night with no school. It was past ten p.m., and if it had been a school night, I'd have had to break out my old trusty trick. I kept a transistor radio (yes, kids, we called them that back then!), stashed away in my bedroom in a secret hiding spot. When I had to go to bed during a Giants game, I'd put that radio under my pillow and listen until I fell asleep or the Giants won. I suspect my mom knew my secret, as at times the radio was sticking out from under the pillow when she came to wake me in the morning. But, being the gold standard of moms, she never said a word. God bless her!

The game headed to the eighth inning, and both pitchers kept dealing blanks. After the scare in the seventh, surprisingly Marichal gained strength. With one out in the eighth, he walked Henry Aaron, prob-

ably not a bad thing to do. Then he retired the next sixteen Braves batters in a row! Who knows what his pitch count was, but the young ace was really dealing now. He finally yielded a harmless single with two outs in the top of the thirteenth but retired the next batter to close out the inning.

The game almost had ended in the bottom of the ninth. Mays led off by hitting a line drive off Spahn, only to have the shortstop throw him out at first. The other Giants Hall of Famer, Willie McCovey, hit a high drive right over the right field foul pole. My favorite umpire (because his name was Chris and he was Greek), Chris Pelekoudas, umping first base, called it foul! Most Giants, including McCovey, thought it was fair. After a heated argument, Stretch bounced out to first. Felipe Alou singled, but Cepeda popped out to third and we were headed for extra innings.

Juan was humming now, setting the Braves down inning after inning. The only problem for the Giants and us faithful fans, both at the game and at home listening, was that the old man, Spahn, was also keeping the Giants scoreless. So as we entered the bottom of the thirteenth, it was still 0–0!

Giants' manager Alvin Dark approached Marichal when he came off the mound after the top of the thirteenth and asked him how he felt. Juan looked out to where Spahn was warming up to pitch the thirteenth inning and broke baseball protocol by telling his manager, "See that old guy out there? He's forty-two! I am not coming out of this game until he does or we win!" With that, Dark shrugged his shoulders and walked away. Marichal admitted after the game that his shoulder was getting stiff in the chill of a typically frigid Candlestick night.

In the bottom of the thirteenth, Spahn gave up a leadoff single to Ernie Bowman, the Giants' light-hitting utility infielder, who had come in for José Pagán at shortstop when Davenport pinch hit for him in the seventh. Finally, a threat! Bowman had speed and was frequently used as a pinch runner. I got excited. Not so fast! Spahn, the wily veteran, promptly picked Bowman off first when he got too big a lead. The next two went down and we were going to the fourteenth in a scoreless tie!

About this time, my dad came in from the garage and asked if the game was still on. I explained the amazing drama unfolding, and he sat down to listen too. It was after eleven p.m. now. A classic was unfolding at The Stick.

Marichal navigated the top of the fourteenth, giving up only his fourth walk. In the bottom of the fourteenth, I thought for sure the Giants would win it. We had Mays and McCovey hitting second and third, with Harvey Kuenn, a former AL batting champion, leading off. Both my dad and I got excited when ol' Harvey, who wound up his career with a .303 batting average, led off with a classic Candlestick windblown double that fell into right field.

This surely was it, the ageless pitcher had to be tiring and we had our version of Murderers'

Row coming up, starting with Mays. Spahn, who Mays had hit more home runs off of than any other pitcher, wisely walked Willie intentionally. But now he had to face the fearsome Willie McCovey, who you might remember had almost won it in the ninth and tied for the home run lead that year with Henry Aaron. I thought for sure the Braves would bring in a relief pitcher. But Bobby Bragan, the Braves manager, probably decided to let his old ace win or lose it on his own.

I was only slightly disappointed when Stretch McCovey fouled out to the catcher. We still had Felipe Alou, a dangerous hitter, and Orlando Cepeda, the Baby Bull, coming up. I was still optimistic. These were two tough right-handed hitters. Both were All-Stars and Cepeda was a future Hall of Famer too. Surely, one of them would win this marathon off the tiring old man on the mound.

But Felipe flied out to shallow center field and both Kuenn and Mays had to hold at second and first. The dangerous Orlando Cepeda was up. Would they dare walk him to load the bases? No! Spahn pitched to Cepeda! He got him to hit a grounder to third, and Menke, who had replaced Eddie Mathews, booted it. Bases loaded now with two outs! Ed Bailey, our powerful catcher, was up now. But he flied out to center field. The crafty old veteran lefty pitched out of it . . . again! How long could this go on?

Marichal set the Braves down again in order in the top of the fifteenth. During the inning, Warren

Spahn batted for himself! Talk about *old-school* baseball! When Marichal came into the dugout after the fifteenth, he noticed Dark had a pitcher warming up in the bullpen. If the Giants could not win it this inning, Juan was probably coming out . . . before the old man!

Spahn, amazingly at this stage, quickly set down the Giants in order in the bottom of the fifteenth. Marichal batted for himself and made the last out by striking out. He was staying in for the sixteenth.

Juan set the Braves down again in the top of the sixteenth, stranding Menke, who had singled with two down. As he left the mound, he waited near first base. Willie Mays for years had the habit of always stepping on first base as he trotted in from center field at the end of an inning. This time Marichal was there waiting. He said to Willie, "Alvin is going to take me out before the old man." Willie just looked at him and said, "Don't worry, I'll end it this inning for you!"

Harvey Kuenn led off the bottom of the inning by flying out to center. I have always wondered this, as Willie Mays dug himself into the batter's box to face Warren Spahn, did he think back to his first home run as a major league player over twelve years before? He'd hit it off none other than the veteran lefty he was about to face now, Spahnie. Willie already had 381 home runs on his odometer and wound up in his career hitting more home runs off Warren Spahn than any other pitcher . . . eighteen! Spahn had to know he was in deep trouble as Mays stood in to face him. But he could not walk the speedy Mays and risk a stolen base. Besides the fearsome HR co-champ that year lurked on deck . . . McCovey.

And so the classic pitchers' duel of the twentieth century finally ended dramatically and suddenly when Mays laced one of Spahn's offerings far over the left field fence and trotted around the bases, as he did 659 other times in his illustrious career. It was simply called a game-winning home run in those long-ago days. It was not until the 1980s that the term "walk-off" came into use. As Willie slowly circled the bases, the old lefty trudged to the locker room. It was over! My dad and I could finally go to bed . . . happy!

We will never see another pitchers' duel like this marathon contest with the starting pitchers going all sixteen innings. With today's emphasis on protecting pitching arms, not to mention protecting multimillion-dollar investments, managers start considering going to the bullpen when a pitcher approaches 90 pitches. Marichal threw 227 and Spahn threw 201 pitches that chilly night at The Stick!

Amazingly, exactly thirty years before, on July 2, 1933, another Giants Hall of Fame pitcher, the great screwball wizard Carl Hubbell, threw an eighteen-inning shutout against the St. Louis Cardinals at the Polo Grounds. He also won 1–0. I rate the Marichal vs. Spahn duel superior because the "candy-ass" Cardinal starting pitcher, Tex Carleton, didn't complete the game and needed relief help after sixteen frames. This was the Cardinal team that would be known a year later as the Gashouse Gang and had many of the same stars.

King Carl Hubbell, as he was known, was probably in attendance the night of the Marichal vs. Spahn duel. He was the Giants' director of the farm system at that time. In 1933 he was 23–12 with a microscopic ERA of 1.66 and won the first of two MVP awards. The Giants won their fourth World Series that year over the Washington Senators in five games. Hubbell won two games and didn't give up an earned run. *King* Carl he most certainly was!

So, this Tuesday night, July 2nd, if you're a baseball fan, give a thought to how the old-timers played our beautiful game fifty years ago. The Marichal vs. Spahn marathon was, in my opinion, the greatest pitching duel of the twentieth century. When pitchers took the ball back then, they expected to finish what they started.

●●●

8 Giants Win Again — 2012 World Series

When the Giants won their second World Championship in San Francisco it was very emotional for me. Here's an e-mail I sent to family and friends that night.

This is going to be a very heart-wrenching message and I apologize to those who may find it a bit too personal. But I have to share this feeling with all of you.

I am still on cloud nine and emotional from last night. Wow! After waiting fifty-two years for the first championship, it feels like the dam has burst and now we have *two* championships in three years! It is as sweet as I always imagined it would be.

There are so many great loyal Giants fans out there. I am not bragging when I claim that I am right at the top of that group. My first Giants game was at six years old at Seals Stadium in their first year in San Francisco, 1958. And I have lived and died with my Giants ever since that first glimpse of the vivid green field and Willie Mays gliding across that emerald expanse. You may find Giants fans *as* loyal as me . . . but I guarantee you will never find one *more* loyal and true to the Giants.

That first championship in 2010 was so sweet and satisfying that I truly thought I'd never experience that kind of euphoria again. But while it never is as good as that first time, in many ways I am more proud and moved by this championship team

this year! As many of you know, I am currently in the fight of my life with Lou Gehrig's Disease, also known as ALS. What I see is a metaphor for my struggle in what this team fought through to win this year.

Just as people wrote off this team when they were down and on the brink of elimination not once, but twice, people have a tendency to write off people with ALS. There's the metaphor I am talking about. Just like me in my fight for my life, this team absolutely refused to give up, even when the odds looked so impossible. And even when they overcame those odds to reach the World Series, all the experts picked them as underdogs to a team that won six fewer games than they did and only had the seventh best record in the American League. But they fought hard and swept the Tigers away in four. So *this* is my favorite Giants team of all time now!

When the 2010 team won the World Series, I was already seriously ill but was able to attend all the post-season games albeit in a wheelchair. This year I am more sick and was not able to attend any games this year. The average survival time for ALS patients is about eighteen months. I was told I had ALS over

three years ago. So I feel fortunate to be around to witness this team win another championship and even to be typing this now.

But, like me, my Giants of 2012 absolutely refused to give up. Barry Zito refused to give up. Ryan Vogelsong refused to give up. And that is a lesson to all of us. It is *never* over until it is over! And that is why this team is my new all-time favorite team.

San Francisco Giants 2012 World Champions of baseball! God, that sounds so great!

•••

9
Giants vs. Dodgers, 1963

Here's a post I wrote for a popular San Francisco Bay Area baseball blog.

In 1963 our next-door neighbors got the first color TV I had ever seen. They bought it mainly because the Giants vs. Dodger games were going to be in *color* for the first time that year. A large gathering was on hand at the neighbors' house to watch that big console RCA color set for the first of those precious nine games at Dodger Stadium, which were the *only TV* games broadcast locally back then.

Remember our Giants were defending NL champs after beating the hated Dodgers in that playoff series the previous October. And their first meeting of the season was on May 10 thru 12 in Dodger Stadium. Well, the Giants were in first place and we all were sure they'd beat the Bums handily and be in many more World Series, never imagining it would be twenty-seven years before the Giants would be in another World Series!!

So that Friday night we all sat down crowded around that miracle of man, a color TV, and were shocked as Drysdale beat Jack Sanford 2–1. Nice color set, nice TV, look at that *green* grass and that *red* infield! But hey, it was only one game!

The next night we sat down to watch Koufax duel Marichal, who was at that time the No. 2 starter behind Sanford. And what does Sandy do? He throws a no-hitter at my beloved Giants! The Dodgers punished us 8–0! I sat there as an ten-year-old and could not believe my idols like Mays, McCovey, Cepeda, and Felipe Alou could not even muster a measly hit against this magician on the mound. How could any human make a curveball do *that*?

The next day, the Dodgers swept us right out of L.A. They went on to win the World Series over the mighty New York Yankees that October!

Thus began my bitter lessons in how "great pitching always beats great hitting!" And believe me, that was a bitter lesson for the next four years until Koufax mercifully retired after 1966!

•••

Willie Mays

This piece was written for a baseball blog in 2013 on the forty-fifth anniversary of Bobby Bonds's sensational debut.

A few people have asked me to write about some of the Giants' history that I have had the pleasure of witnessing these past fifty-six years of Giants baseball in San Francisco. Here is a story about a very memorable moment in that history. I hope you enjoy it!

This Tuesday our Giants will be playing the Dodgers. It is also the 45th anniversary of Bobby Bonds's debut, which was against the Dodgers also on a Tuesday night. And what a debut it was! In Bobby Bonds's first game in the big leagues, he made an instant impact on this heated age-old Giants vs. Dodgers rivalry.

I think younger Giants fans would like to know the context of this debut and older Orange-and-Black fans be reminded of a sweet memory. The Giants were in the midst of being bridesmaids for five straight years. They were again chasing the defending champions, the St. Louis Cardinals, for the elusive pennant. 1968 was rightly called the "Year of the Pitcher." The slugging Giants with Hall of Famers Mays and McCovey plus slugger Jim Ray Hart barely hit 100 HRs that season. Pitching that season was so dominant that the League ERA for the NL was 2.99. After the season, to boost offense, baseball lowered the mound from fifteen inches to where it is today, ten inches.

Bobby Bonds had been tearing up the Pacific Coast League that spring. He was batting a cool .370 with an OPS of over 1,000. I remember following his progress weekly in *The Sporting News*, at that time truly the bible of baseball. It was merely a matter of time for him to get called up. And that call came on June 25, 1968.

The Giants were opening up a thirteen-game home stand at The Stick against the hated Bums from L.A. So it was with much interest that we all waited to see what this phenom Bobby Bonds could do. Could he boost the offense to give us a chance against the Cards this summer?

The pitching match-up was a pair of stylish lefties, Claude Osteen for the Dodgers and the much maligned by Giants fans Ray Sadecki. Most of us Giants fans had not forgiven poor Sadecki for being the player who was acquired for our beloved "Baby Bull," Orlando Cepeda, two years before.

All Orlando did in 1967, the year after that trade, was win the NL MVP unanimously and lead the Cardinals over the second-place Giants to the World Championship!

We did not care that Sadecki was having two good years as a Giant. He went 12–6 in 1967 with a sub 3 ERA. This Year of the Pitcher he actually again had a good 2.78 ERA and threw six shutouts. But runs were so scarce in 1968, even on the slugging Giants, he led the NL that year with eighteen losses (and recent Giants fans used to fret over Matt Cain not receiving run support)! This night he was to throw the best game of his Giants career: a two-hit shutout with ten Ks!

But all attention was on the twenty-two-year-old Bonds making his debut in the seven hole that night. Going to the sixth, Bobby had grounded to short in his first AB and then got plunked by Osteen in the fifth. But even that helped the Giants score as it loaded the bases with no outs and they tallied when Hal Lanier hit into a DP.

It was Giants 1–0 going to the bottom of the sixth. Sadecki had only given up one hit, a double to the pitcher Osteen in the third while striking out seven! In the sixth, the Giants started to get to Osteen. The ex-Dodger and new Giant that year, Ron Hunt, led off with a single. He moved to third on a double by Jesús Alou. Then the Dodgers walked McCovey to load the bases and pitch to Mays! Yes, you read that right; they walked McCovey, a lefty-lefty match-up, to pitch to the best ballplayer in history in my opinion . . . Willie Mays!

Fans today do not realize what terror Willie "Stretch" McCovey struck in the hearts of baseball managers back in his prime, even in the Year of the Pitcher. How did it work out for the Dodgers? Osteen walked Mays to force in a run and make it 2–0. The Dodgers' manager, Walter Alston, went to the bullpen for John Purdin, a hard-throwing right-hander with some promise. Purdin promptly walked Jim Ray Hart to force in a third run, and it was 3–0. Still none out and bases juiced.

Purdin rallied and struck out Jack Hiatt. One out, bases loaded, and here came the rookie Bobby Bonds to the plate. Could he ice the game for the Giants and make it a blowout? Could he! He laced a Purdin pitch out of The Stick, wind be damned, for a grand slam in his first game in the majors! Giants 7, Dodgers 0, and joy all around Northern California for those who heard Lon Simmons say, "Tell it *good-bye*!" Game to the Giants, especially with Sadecki blanking the Bums that night.

So that is the way the super-talented Bobby Bonds broke into the majors that Tuesday night forty-five years ago, in the midst of the Year of the Pitcher and against our blood rivals, the Dodgers. Barry's daddy could play some ball also! This Tuesday night, give a thought to the late Bobby Bonds and maybe tip your Giants cap that I'm sure you have on.

•••

11 *F. Robby*

Hall of Famer and Oakland native
Frank Robinson

Here's a posting on a popular San Francisco Bay Area baseball blog on Frank Robinson's seventy-eight birthday in 2013.

I thought that today, Frank Robinson's 78th birthday, would be a good time to tell you my F. Robby story.

In 1975 I worked as a rookie computer programmer in Oakland right across the Nimitz Freeway from the Coliseum. I used to go to the Edgewater Hyatt hotel frequently for lunch, as it was a short walk from my office on Edgewater Drive.

All the sports teams who played in Oakland back then stayed at the Hyatt, and I ran into a lot of my sports heroes there at lunch. One day I chatted with Kareem Abdul-Jabbar there!

Well, one fine spring day in 1975, I was enjoying my patty melt, which they did great at the Hyatt. Who sits down right across from my table at the next table? Frank Robinson, the first African American manager in major league history and a local Oakland guy! Not to mention he was one of the great stars I used to go see at Candlestick back in the early 1960s, before he was traded by the Reds in 1965 because they thought he was an "old" thirty. Talk about a *stupid* trade!

I got excited not only by seeing one of my childhood idols this close. But also because literally minutes before I had just read in the *Sporting Green* that Dennis Eckersley was starting his first game as a major leaguer tomorrow! Though Eck was two

45

years younger than me, we'd played ball against one another in Fremont where we both grew up. He was only one year behind me in high school and youth baseball leagues.

Frank did not look like he was in a pleasant mood. But I just had to say something to him! So I gathered up my courage and said, "Mr. Robinson, I see Eckersley is making his first major league start tomorrow against the A's." Frank looked up like he had swallowed a lemon with his lunch and, chewing, said nothing. So undaunted I continued, "I played baseball against Eckersley in Fremont, right down the road!"

Frank finally spoke up and said, "How'd you do against him?"

"Not well, although I recall one off-field bloop double off him. He was damned hard to hang in there for a right-hander batter like me!" I said.

Frank smiled and munched his lunch for a moment, and said, "You've put on a few pounds since you played ball!"

I blushed. The four years since high school and marriage had not been kind to my midsection for sure. "Yeah, I am afraid so, Mr. Robinson."

Frank laughed a bit and then said, "By the way, Eckersley is not pitching tomorrow."

Flustered, I blurted out one of the stupidest comments of my life—"But the paper says he's going tomorrow, Frank"—as I pointed to the article in the *Sporting Green*.

He thought this was either a joke or a challenge to his authority and giving me an icy stare, he said, "I am the manager, and I say he's not starting tomorrow! Who you going to believe, the newspaper or me?"

I stammered, "Okay, Mr. Robinson! So Eckersley is not pitching in the series at all then?"

"He's pitching Sunday," he said.

So with the ice broken, Frank and I had a nice conversation for a half hour or so. We talked about his days in Oakland and who my favorite ballplayer was. Of course, he thought I made an excellent choice in making my idol Willie Mays!

That was my one and only meeting with Hall of Famer Frank Robinson. Oh, and how did the local kid from Fremont do on Sunday? Eck threw a three-hit shutout against the three-time World Champion A's is all! And whom did he beat in that game? His former teammate, Jim Perry, whom the Indians had traded to the A's for Blue Moon Odom only six days before! Who was Jim Perry, you ask? He is the older brother of Giants and Indians great Gaylord Perry. He in fact was the first Perry brother to win a Cy Young in 1970 with the Twins. They are the only brothers to win Cy Young Awards.

That was Jim Perry's last few months in baseball as a pitcher. The A's released him a few months later that season. So here was a twenty-year-old future Hall of Famer, Eck, starting his brilliant career by beating the team he would star for as the first

"closer." And a fine pitcher, Jim Perry was, ending a nice ML career! Baseball has so many inner stories. That is why we love it so much, I guess.

Duane Kuiper was a twenty-three-year-old rookie on that team, too. He was called up to the Indians for good a week or so after Eck threw his shutout. Oh, and I seem to remember seeing a skinny Kuip roaming around the Edgewater Hyatt House back in those days, too!

• • •

Jim Ray Hart (top) with
Tom Haller (bottom) run down Lou Brock

I really enjoyed your interviews with Nate Oliver and Johnny Antonelli! You're the greatest at getting former players to open up and tell their best stories. I know you pride yourself on getting your baseball history right so I'll correct a minor error you made when talking about Jim Ray Hart getting hit by Bob Gibson in Jimmy Ray's debut.

You said, incorrectly, that Gibson broke Jim Ray Hart's shoulder blade after he hit a home run off Gibson. Let me tell you how it happened.

I remember it vividly as my father and I were listening to the game while my father worked in the garage. My grandfather and father wanted to see Stan "The Man" Musial in his final year. They tried to get tickets for the doubleheader on Sunday. But it was sold out! Instead, we went to the Saturday game and saw the Giants win. But back to Jim Ray Hart vs. Bob Gibson.

It was a Sunday doubleheader against the Cardinals at Candlestick on July 7, 1963, the last day before the All-Star break. It was Jim Ray Hart's debut that day. We'd heard a lot about Jim Ray Hart in Tacoma and his call-up was greatly anticipated.

12 *Painful Debut*

The Giants won the first game in fifteen innings, and Jimmy Ray broke in with two hits in his first MLB game. The second game was a match-up of two greats, Hall of Fame pitchers Juan Marichal and Bob Gibson. Juan was coming off his famous sixteen-inning classic vs. Warren Spahn five days prior (see "Pitching Duel for the Ages," page 36). Giants manager Alvin Dark had generously given Juan a whole extra day's rest after his historic marathon! Boy, times were surely different back then.

The infamous Gibson beaning took place in the second inning of the second game. It was Hart's first time facing Gibson. That's when Gibson broke Hart's shoulder with a fastball up and in. Alvin Dark called it a disgrace. Ernie Bowman, the next batter after Hart's injury, also got dusted by Gibson. I remember my dad saying Gibson was as bad a headhunter as Drysdale after Bowman got low bridged.

The next inning, when Gibson came up, Juan dusted him good! He got fined fifty dollars for that. Nowadays he'd be tossed! Gibson wound up shutting out the Giants 5–0. How did Juan do in the game after his masterpiece against Spahn? He shut out the Cardinals until one down in the seventh when Stan "The Man" himself hit a two-run homer off him! It was Musial's final home run against the Giants. Stan "The Man" owned the Giants . . . he hit 89 of his 475 career home runs off Giants pitchers. His home run off the Dominican Dandy also broke a string of 30⅓ innings of not allowing an earned run by Marichal.

There's actually film of Gibson breaking Jimmy Ray's shoulder blade in the outstanding new documentary *Fastball*, narrated by Kevin Costner. It's at 26 minutes, 35 seconds into the movie. I highly recommend this great baseball documentary! It's on Netflix for streaming, if you have it. There's also a great still image of Mays being drilled in the back by Gibson. It had to be later in Willie's career, as when he was younger, his reflexes made him extremely difficult to hit, even for a hard thrower like Gibson!

So that's the saga of Jimmy Ray Hart's debut. Thanks to the excellent baseball-reference.com, I was able to verify my memories and expand them.

I'm copying Bruce Jenkins also, as I know he's also interested in baseball history. Keep up the great work, Marty! You're the best!

Tony Gwynn's classic stroke

13
"Wait Until You See This Kid!"

This story was posted on a popular baseball blog in 2014 when Tony Gwynn passed. Gwynn was not only a great batter with eight NL batting titles, but he also won five Gold Glove Awards for his play in right field. He also stole over three hundred bases in his illustrious twenty-year career.

It was with a heavy, heavy heart that I heard of the passing of the great Hall of Famer Tony Gwynn today. He was a great ballplayer and from all accounts a better human being! I was reminded of the first time I saw him play. He made a stunningly immediate impact on me years ago. Which is why I thought I'd share this story. I hope you enjoy it. Writing is not easy for me nowadays, and it took me all day to write.

Back in the mid-1970s until the mid-'80s I worked as an IT specialist for Levi Strauss & Co. here in San Francisco. I worked in the warehouse support area and Levi's had two big warehouses, along with a few manufacturing plants in Amarillo, Texas. Because of this, I spent more than my share of time in Amarillo. My trips there would last weeks, and in two cases months!

Now Levi's was a great place to work back then, and I loved working in my native San Francisco. But my road trips to Amarillo . . . I must admit were my least favorite thing about working there. Not to pile on, but how can you compare a High Plains cow town with some of the worst weather and smells with one of the most beautiful cities in the world? Trips to Amarillo became one of the necessary evils of my job.

I worked a lot of overtime at work in Amarillo. Two things made this desirable: 1) There was not a heck of a lot to do there unless it involved bars and chasing cowgirls, and I must plead guilty to pursuing that sport more than I should have; 2) And this was the most critical reason to work around the clock, it meant getting out of there as fast as possible!

I did find a pretty good Greek restaurant in town on the old Route 66, Amarillo Blvd., Nick's Restaurant, founded by the current owner's father when there was steady traffic down Route 66. I frequented the place often, as I got tired of huge steaks and greasy chicken fried steak after awhile.

The owner Alex found out I was Greek, and we hit it off. I always got huge portions of all the Greek specialties he would make for me. Special because the only thing he could sell in Amarillo were gyros and cheeseburgers—although all the local folks mispronounced the gyros like a spinning device that guided airplanes! Alex also had a beautiful daughter, Eleni, my age, who had a big crush on me and I'm sure that influenced my frequent visits, too!

Alex found out that we had something else in common besides our Greek heritage; we both loved baseball! He had two season tickets right behind home plate for the local AA team, the Amarillo Gold Sox, who were a Padres affiliate. We went to many games together on some hot summer nights, especially when the Giants' AA team, the Shreveport Captains, was in town. I loved seeing the future Giants. Also, it kept me out of the bars and chasing cowgirls . . . at least for a few hours!

The Giants had once had an AA affiliate in town, the Amarillo Giants. I remember devouring my weekly *Sporting News*, the "baseball bible" back in the day, and tracking future Giants like Dave Kingman and Jim Barr, who both passed through Amarillo on their way to the San Francisco Giants.

On a hot summer night, Alex and I headed out to see the visiting Shreveport Captains take on the hometown Amarillo Gold Sox. It was 1981 and on the way to the park, Alex raved about this kid who had just joined the Gold Sox a few weeks before. He was tearing up the Texas League, a left-handed batter with speed—his name was, of course, Tony Gwynn. The Gold Sox were in a race for the division title, and it was the last week of the season. As I drove, Alex read the stats to me from the paper of this phenom; he was hitting over .400. Of course, as I said, it was only a couple of weeks. But Alex said wait till I saw his stroke!

When the game started, I was impressed by the stylish lefty that set down the Captains in short order. His name was Dave Dravecky, a future favorite Giant. He struck out my favorite Shreveport player, whom I'd followed since coming out of San Jose—that was Danny Gladden, another future popular Giant.

In the bottom of the first, I was especially following the Captains' right-hander starting that night, another future Giant, Alan Fowlkes, who I'd seen pitch a fine game earlier that summer in Amarillo. Alex elbowed me as Gwynn stepped in. On one of the first pitches, he hit a bullet, a searing liner to right center for a double. Alex gushed, "This kid's a *player*! Did you see that stroke?" I did see it

and was immediately impressed!

To shorten this story just a bit, the Gold Sox won in a rout, something like 11–2. Tony Gwynn hit ropes you could hang laundry on all over the field, going 5 for 5 with two doubles, the second one missing being a homer by a foot or two. He threw in a stolen base for good measure! Dravecky pitched great, only giving up a homer to John Rabb, the Captains' catcher. . . . I always followed the catchers, being a member of the catchers' fraternity myself.

The years sure proved my dear, late Greek friend Alex right. The kid was a player all right, all the way into Cooperstown. Tony finished that 1981 season in Amarillo hitting .462, and next season he was in San Diego giving my Giants, not to mention my buddy Mike Krukow, fits for years to come on his way to the Hall of Fame!

I've been to numerous minor league games over the years and nobody ever made such a strong impression on me like the great Tony Gwynn did that steamy August night in Amarillo thirty-three years ago. I just had to share this story with my baseball friends.

Baseball lost a jewel in Tony Gwynn, tragically way too young. I never had the pleasure to meet you in person, but you made a big impression the first time I saw you play the game we both love! Rest in peace, Mr. Gwynn.

•••

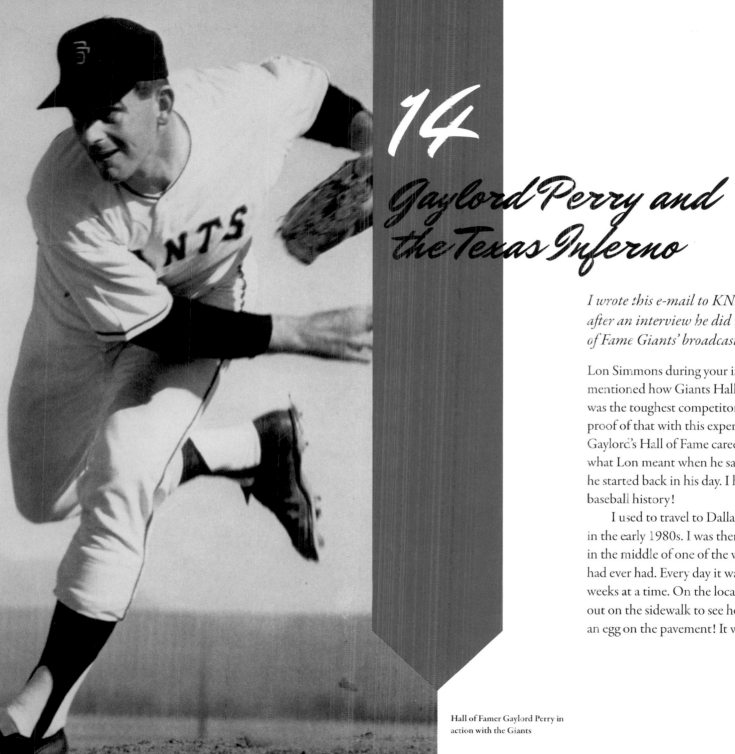

14

Gaylord Perry and the Texas Inferno

I wrote this e-mail to KNBR's Marty Lurie after an interview he did with the late Hall of Fame Giants' broadcaster Lon Simmons.

Lon Simmons during your interview today mentioned how Giants Hall of Famer Gaylord Perry was the toughest competitor he ever saw. Well, I have proof of that with this experience at the tail end of Gaylord's Hall of Fame career. Here is an example of what Lon meant when he said Gaylord finished what he started back in his day. I hope you enjoy this bit of baseball history!

I used to travel to Dallas a lot on business back in the early 1980s. I was there in June of 1980 right in the middle of one of the worst heat waves they had ever had. Every day it was reaching 115 or so, for weeks at a time. On the local news, they were going out on the sidewalk to see how long it took to cook an egg on the pavement! It was brutal heat!

Hall of Famer Gaylord Perry in action with the Giants

A fellow manager at Levi Strauss, where I worked, had excellent season tix for the Rangers at the old Arlington ballpark. He asked me if I wanted his two tix, as it was just too hot for him to go that night. It was 115 outside when he offered them to me. But I had read in the morning papers that ol' Gaylord Perry, one of my 1960s Giants idols, was starting that night for the Rangers vs. the Twins. So even though it was extremely hot, I took the tix and even found a young Texas beauty to accompany me to the game that night . . . but that is another story.

I wanted to go because I love baseball, but also for nostalgia's sake to see my old Giants idol Gaylord pitch one last time. He was forty-one, and I figured he wouldn't last long that night in the brutal heat. At game time, the temp was an unreal 109! So, what did ol' Gaylord do that night in that absolute steam bath? He threw a four-hit shutout at the Twins!

It was the gutsiest pitching performance I have ever seen. Although, I am sure all that perspiration greatly assisted Gaylord's "specialty" pitches that night.

When the game was over, as our seats were right behind the Rangers' dugout, I got to chat with Gaylord for a moment as he waited to be interviewed. I told him I was an old Giants fan that had seen him pitch as a kid in the '60s. He tipped his cap and said, "Then that was for *you*!" One of my most memorable baseball memories! And the rest of the evening was not too bad either.

•••

15 R.I.P., Jim Ray Hart

Upon hearing of Jim Ray Hart's passing in 2016, I sent this e-mail to baseball friends.

I was very saddened to hear of Jim Ray Hart's passing yesterday. He was one of my favorite Giants back when I literally lived and breathed baseball in the 1960s. I was young, and he came up right as I was intensely following the Giants. I was reading *The Sporting News*, which in those times truly was the "baseball bible." He was probably the second-best hitting third baseman after Matt Williams in San Francisco Giants history, in my opinion.

His debut was dramatically tragic. On his first day in the big leagues on July 7, 1963, during the nightcap of a Sunday doubleheader, the meanest pitcher this side of Don Drysdale, Bob Gibson, broke his shoulder blade! By the way, there's an excellent new documentary, *Fastball*, which is available online on Netflix and on DVD. In the part about Bob Gibson, there's brief video of him breaking Jim Ray Hart's shoulder. I would highly recommend this documentary about fastballs . . . as we know, speed kills! Get a hold of it either online or on DVD. (See "Painful Debut" on page 47 to find out more about Hart's debut.)

In 1964, Jim Ray was up for good. He had a stellar rookie season with thirty-one homers. If it

weren't for the notorious East Coast press bias, he would've won the NL Rookie of the Year Award that instead went to Richie Allen (later known as Dick Allen). Late in the 1964 season, he had another dramatic bit of misfortune that's described next.

Back in the '60s, the Giants vs. Dodgers rivalry was downright nasty, even more so than the last twenty years. They truly hated one another! Remember the infamous incident when Juan Marichal took a bat to John Roseboro in 1965? Well, the year before, in '64, there was another incident. It was in a game we watched on TV from Dodger Stadium. Back then, we only got the nine games from L.A. on TV. I remember it was also one of the first color broadcasts we watched on our family's first color TV! I remember marveling at how red the infield dirt was. The Dodgers used crushed brick for the infield back then. The vivid scarlet red infield in contrast to the bright green grass, along with the blue and orange/black uniforms . . . we were in awe of color TV!

During the game, the Giants' slugging rookie third baseman Jim Ray Hart was coming into second base to break up a double play. Now Jimmy Ray was

San Francisco Giants All-Star
Jim Ray Hart

a hell of a hitter with tremendous power, but he was not known as the smartest player around. On this play, the ball was hit hard to shortstop. The Dodgers' shortstop, Maury Wills, had plenty of time to step on second base and fire to first for an easy double play. But Jimmy Ray, who was closing in on second, did not get down early enough and the Dodgers' fiery shortstop drilled him right in the forehead!

The ball knocked Jimmy Ray out cold instantly and bounced halfway into right field. We thought he was dead, the way he dropped like a sniper had shot him and how the ball bounced all that way. They carried him off on a stretcher and to the hospital. He was only out a few days. Today he would've been out at least a month.

And guess who replaced Jim Ray at third base after his getting drilled on the bases? Willie Mays! Yep, he could do it all and often did for the Giants. It was Willie's first time playing third. Earlier that season Willie, the perennial Gold Glove winner and the best center fielder of all time, had played shortstop in the famous twenty-three-inning game vs. the Mets in the brand new Shea Stadium. That was the second game of a doubleheader and remains the longest doubleheader in MLB history timewise.

Let me end this tribute with a more pleasant memory of Jim Ray's tremendous power. I wrote this after Lon Simmons's passing last year.

Lon's trademark call of, "You can tell it *good-bye*!" for a Giants home run was a takeoff on his partner Russ's call of, "Tell it 'Bye, Bye, Baby!'" Both of them got to make their famous home run calls frequently with such sluggers as Hall of Famers Willie Mays, Willie McCovey, and Orlando Cepeda on the Giants then! All three of them led the league at least once in home runs in the '60s. Yet it was not for any of these famous sluggers that I recall Lon calling a home run more vividly than this home run hit by the fine slugging third baseman, Jim Ray Hart.

I was at the game with my dear father. It was at a game in 1966, before Candlestick was fully enclosed by the upper deck, as was done for the 49ers when they moved to The Stick in 1971. It was a typical Candlestick Park bitterly cold night game. The famous Candlestick wind was blowing around Candlestick Hill and in from left field. It was a fierce gale that night.

When the Giants moved to Candlestick in 1960, Willie Mays had adjusted his swing to hit to right where the winds assisted fly balls. Orlando Cepeda had a natural inside-out swing with his closed stance and hit many home runs to right center at Candlestick. But Jim Ray Hart was a dead pull hitter who had tremendous power to the left side. He hit vicious line drives that you could hang laundry on!

My father and I could hear the multitude of transistor radios in the crowd as Russ and Lon called the game from the KSFO radio booth. Back then, it was common to see people all over downtown listening to their transistor radios to hear Russ and Lon broadcast the game. Men would sneak in a small transistor radio to the opera or ballet and listen to Lon and Russ through tiny earplugs.

As Jim Ray Hart dug in and took his stance in the batter's box, both Russ and Lon mentioned how strong the wind was blowing in from left. Lon, who was doing the play-by-play, said, "With this hurricane force wind blowing in from left tonight, Russ, I don't think we'll be seeing any balls hit out to left tonight." No sooner had those words left his lips, with Russ quickly agreeing, than Jimmy Ray connected with a thunderous crack! Lon: "There's a deep fly ball to left . . . way back! . . . way back! . . . you can tell it *good-bye*!"

The ball was hit so hard on a line, like a 3 iron in golf, that it was still rising as it crossed the chain-link fence in left field. After chuckling along with Russ, Lon said, "That's how much we know about baseball, Russ! Maybe I should say that each time Jimmy Ray comes to bat!"

That was Jim Ray Hart, a great power hitting player on those power hitting Giants' teams of the '60s. Perhaps he was overshadowed by the Hall of Fame sluggers Willie Mays, Willie McCovey, and Orlando Cepeda to the casual fans. But not to this young diehard Giants fan! He was truly one of my favorite players! Good-bye, Jim Ray. This fan will not forget when you were young, strong, and struck fear in the hearts of NL pitchers . . . it doesn't seem that long ago!

Rest in peace, Jim Ray.

●●●

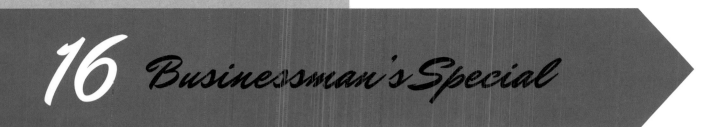

Candlestick Park (The Stick) before the outfield was enclosed for the San Francisco 49ers in 1971

Here's another posting to a San Francisco Bay Area baseball blog about a game where I almost got tossed out of The Stick by my least favorite umpire . . . no kidding!

In 1968, known as the Year of the Pitcher, Don Drysdale of the Dodgers broke Walter "Big Train" Johnson's fifty-five-year-old consecutive scoreless innings record. The Giants and an umpire played key roles in Drysdale setting the record. Going into a big three-game series in L.A., the Giants hoped to maintain or extend their slim 1½ game lead over the Braves for first place. The Dodgers were just trying to get to .500.

It happened in Dodger Stadium as I was watching as a fifteen-year-old kid. To be precise, it was the day after Memorial Day on May 31st, a Friday night game. Yes, kids, until 1971, Memorial Day was celebrated on May 30th regardless of what day of the week that date fell. Back then, the only Giants games we got on TV were the nine Giants games at Dodger Stadium and the odd Game of the Week, *if* it was on the road!

Drysdale was closing in on Giants' Hall of Famer Carl Hubbell, who had fired 45⅓ innings of consecutive blanks in 1933. King Carl's record was considered the modern record because Walter Johnson's record from 1913 was during baseball's "dead ball" era. In a fascinating twist, Hubbell was the director of the Giants' farm system that night as Don "Big D" Drysdale took the mound.

Drysdale shut out the Giants through eight innings, and the scoreless innings streak stood at forty-three innings entering the ninth. The Giants quickly loaded the bases with no outs. Up to the plate stepped Dick Dietz, the seventh-place hitter. With the Giants only trailing 3–0, not only was the scoreless streak in jeopardy, but also the game. On a 2–2 count, Drysdale threw a slider high and inside. Dietz threw his arm up to protect himself, and the ball hit his left arm. I jumped up to shout gleefully, "That's it! The streak's over, Drysdale!" I was totally stupefied when the home plate umpire made an unfamiliar gesture and called Dietz back from his jog to first. My Dad and I sat there in silence as Lon Simmons and Russ Hodges tried to decipher what was going on.

When it was clear that home plate ump Harry Wendelstedt was claiming Dietz made no effort to avoid getting hit by the pitch, my dad and I yelled in righteous indignation that the call was *bush*! Rather than a run being forced in and a 3–1 game, it was a ball to run the count full. Harry Wendelstedt had his own delusional idea of what had happened. My father said it was the worst "homer" call he'd ever seen! I was inconsolable, shouting at the TV as Giants manager Herman Franks got tossed for his animated tirade over the horrible call.

In the end, it was ruled ball three and with the count now full, Dietz popped out to short left field. It was much too short for pinch runner Nate Oliver to score from third. I howled at the TV and my mother came rushing in to find out what all the commotion was about. We told her the Giants had been robbed with the worst call in baseball history! She shrugged, said "too bad," and went back to the kitchen.

Ty Cline, a utility outfielder who batted lefty, pinch hit for light-hitting righty Hal Lanier. Ty grounded to first baseman Wes Parker, a slick fielding Gold Glover, who came home to force out Nate Oliver. My outrage grew, as now it would take a base hit or a Dodger mistake to break the streak. An extra base hit could tie it up! Jack Hiatt, who is still working for the Giants at the time of this writing, pinch hit for the pitcher Mike McCormick. I was on the edge of my seat with nervousness and mounting outrage.

Jack Hiatt was one of my favorite Giants. He was a catcher, the same position I played. He had power and could put us ahead with a grand slam. In a game we attended at The Stick in April, he had hit a triple off Drysdale and a homer off Jim Brewer. That game was curiously also a match-up of McCormick and Drysdale, which the Giants won 3–0.

Now unless Hiatt did something here, we would lose by that same score! Being the ever-optimistic teenager, I reminded my father of Jack's grand slam the previous year off the Pirates' fine relief ace, Elroy Face. I didn't forget grand slams back then. With

another grand slammer here, he could put us ahead! C'mon, Jack, hit it out off this bum!

Hiatt popped out to Parker at first to end the game. I sat still for a moment and then erupted with some choice cuss words! My father just shook his head and repeated that was the worst call he had ever seen. My dear mother rushed in to demand I watch my mouth around my younger siblings! Final score: 3–0 Dodgers.

Four days later, tragically, on the very night Drysdale surpassed Carl Hubbell's record to set the modern MLB record, Bobby Kennedy was assassinated in L.A. Those days are seared into my memory like it was yesterday! The despised Don Drysdale, who had a nasty habit of knocking down my idol Willie Mays for years, went on to set the major league record for scoreless innings at fifty-eight. Another despised Dodgers pitcher, Orel Hershiser, broke Drysdale's record twenty years later with fifty-nine consecutive scoreless frames, a record that still stands today.

Fast forward nine years later to August 1977. I was working for Levi Strauss in downtown San Francisco as a computer programmer. I'd been working on a long, grueling project in Amarillo, Texas. Our project team had just returned from a miserable two weeks in Amarillo, and we were scheduled to return the following Monday. We'd put in one-hundred-hour work weeks while there. Amarillo was by far my least favorite travel destination! Under the circumstances, to make up for the many hours of unpaid overtime, we could get some compensatory time off. Being a baseball fanatic, I chose a day game during the week as my time off.

I chose that afternoon for a ball game not merely because I could take the time off. I wanted to go see one of my childhood Giants idols, Willie McCovey. "Stretch" was having a late-career resurgence that year after rejoining the Giants. Big Mac had been exiled for three years, first to San Diego then, of all places, Oakland for the final month of 1976. I never got used to seeing Stretch in any colors other than Giants' orange and black. He looked particularly out of place in the green and gold of Charlie Finley's A's!

Willie McCovey was rejuvenated at age thirty-nine that year by being back where he belonged. He hit twenty-eight homers, his final season of twenty or more. He drove in eighty-six and hit .280. It wasn't surprising that he finished a respectable twentieth in the NL MVP voting that fall.

I also wanted to see Ed Halicki pitch that afternoon. Nicknamed "Ho Ho" for his six-foot-seven-inch height, Halicki was one of the Giants' promising hard-throwing young pitchers. Along with John "The Count" Montefusco, Bob Knepper, and the "old man at twenty-nine" Jim Barr, the Giants had the makings of a formidable staff for years to come. In fact, the following year, 1978, with the addition of Vida Blue the Giants made a good run at the Dodgers, the NL Champions that year. That summer *The Sporting News*, the "baseball bible," featured a great color cover photo of Vida, Montefusco, Knepper, and Barr with the Golden Gate Bridge in the background.

Halicki had tossed a no-hitter at the Mets two years before, in 1979, at Candlestick. That was the last no-hitter at home for a Giants pitcher for thirty-four long years. Jonathan Sánchez broke the long drought in 2009. Curiously, forty years after Halicki's no-no, in 2015 Chris Heston no-hit the Mets, but in New York. I'd never seen a MLB no-hitter in person, and I was hoping for a repeat no-hit performance by Halicki.

Back then, the Giants played more weekday day games because The Stick was only for diehard fans during night games! During extra innings of night games, the Giants gave out Croix de Candlestick pins to those hardy fans who remained to brave the frigid winds and cold temps of The Stick. Being a confirmed diehard fan, I earned my share of those prized pins. It was like a badge of honor to have numerous Croix sitting proudly on your Giants cap!

The Giants called some of these weekday day games Businessman's Specials. Businessman's Specials started a bit earlier so businessmen could stretch their lunch hour and take in a game. Back then, games rarely lasted three hours unless there were extra innings. At twenty-four, I didn't feel like the typical "businessman." But I'd definitely earned the time off with my two weeks of overtime in Amarillo, and the ballpark was my natural habitat. I always get a thrill, even today, walking into a ballpark and seeing the diamond with its emerald green turf, albeit detestable Astroturf in those days at The Stick.

I didn't have a ticket. But in those days, that wasn't a problem at all! The Giants during those lean years were one of the worst teams in attendance. That year, 1977, the Giants finished dead last in NL attendance. The previous year, in 1976, the team had nearly moved to Toronto!

Like in 1992, the Giants were saved by last-minute "white knights." In 1976, the white knights were prominent real estate tycoon Bob Lurie from San Francisco and his partner, cattleman Bud Herseth from Phoenix. As I headed to The Stick on the Muni ballpark express from the old Transbay Terminal, I wasn't worried at all about a ticket. No worries about paying astronomical StubHub prices back then.

When I got to the ticket window, I nailed a box seat right behind home plate in the second row for less than ten dollars! I grabbed a beer, dog, and bag of peanuts on my way to my seat. My total cost at that point? Less than twenty dollars! Going to a baseball game was certainly easier on the wallet in 1977!

It was a clear blue-sky August day that's typical for the Bay Area in the summer. As I settled into my primo seat, I took off my tie and suit jacket. It was warm enough in the sun at that time of day. The brisk winds that made Candlestick Park infamous usually appeared in the late afternoon. The beer was cold from the first long, satisfying quaff. It sure hit the spot on a sunny day at "The Yard." There's two things that never taste as good as at The Yard: beer and hot dogs! I looked forward to a few hours of enjoyment watching my favorite team play my favorite sport.

When they showed the umpires for the game on the scoreboard, imagine my surprise when I discovered Harry Wendelstedt was behind the plate for the game! The memory of his atrocious call that enabled Drysdale to set the scoreless innings record in 1968 still incensed me. And here I was, easily within earshot of the scoundrel who made that pathetic hometown call. Immediately I shouted in my best deep masculine voice, "You're a bum, Wendelstedt!" just to stretch out my vocal cords. Harry turned to see who was riding him even before the first pitch.

Well, I was young and strong-voiced back then. As the game progressed, I proceeded to really let Harry have it. "Hey, Harry! Did Drysdale share his bogus record with you?" was one of my favorite taunts. Harry heard me loud and clear, as there were only about four thousand at the game that day. They were playing the Astros. I remember the Giants' young catcher Gary Alexander got a kick out of me riding Harry and he even hit a home run that day!

The beer was having its effect on me about the sixth inning. My inhibitions dulled by four beers, I kept up my ragging on Wendelstedt. Young catcher Alexander's two-run homer had put the Giants ahead 4–2 at the end of four. The Astros fought back to tie it up in the fifth. The Giants took the lead back 5–4 in the bottom of the fifth. Halicki was done after six innings, with the Giants still clinging to the 5–4 lead. Our ace reliever, the usually lights-out lefty Gary Lavelle, started the seventh.

Lavelle had been our bullpen ace for the last few years. In 1977, he was our lone representative in Yankee Stadium at the All-Star game. He had pitched two scoreless innings in the National League's victory. He entered the game with a sparkling ERA of 1.47! I was confident he would close out the Astros for the final three innings and my afternoon off would be rewarded with a victory. I began to let up on Harry as I basked in the lead and sun, along with an increasingly pleasant buzz from the suds.

Instead, Lavelle got bombed, giving up three runs before Randy Moffitt extinguished the flames. Moffitt was the younger brother of famous ladies' tennis player Billie Jean King. We trailed now 7–5, entering the bottom of the seventh. There was still plenty of time for a comeback victory. But my mood had changed witnessing the torching of Lavelle, and I lit into Harry with renewed vigor!

After I questioned Harry's eyesight, judgment, and whether he had on his blue Dodgers shorts, between innings Harry approached me in the stands. I stood up to yell more insults as he closed in. In a calm, half-amused voice, he said, "Young man, you've had too much beer and if you don't stop your disturbance, I'll toss you out of here!"

I laughed. "Why? Can't you take the truth, Wendelstedt! That call in 1968 was total BS, Harry, and you know it! Besides, I haven't used any profanities." Harry's face reddened as I had dragged out his last name for effect.

He smirked and added, "You're close to getting tossed! Now sit down and watch baseball. If I hear one more insult, you're gone!" He got mad and the vein on his neck stuck out halfway through his warning to me.

Not wanting to get my afternoon in the sun cut short, I sat down and bit my tongue for two and a half innings. I wasn't drunk enough to lose my sense of danger. Two guys behind me who had had more beer than me tried to egg me on. "Don't let him have the last word! All Giants fans know that was a BS call! Let him have it, guy!" they half laughed, as they egged me on. I almost made their day and stood up to yell what surely would've been my final insult at Harry.

Just then, an older, well-dressed woman seated next to me, who had been quietly watching me in amusement the whole game, said, "Don't get thrown out, son. Sit down and watch the Giants come back to win!" She smiled and gently tugged my arm as she said this. I sat down. Saved by a wise voice of reason at the last moment!

When one of my idols, Willie McCovey, flied out to center field to end the game in a loss, I couldn't stand it. I shouted a loud stream of final, sore loser insults at Wendelstedt. He ignored me and walked towards the right field exit from the field. I thanked the nice older woman for saving my butt from getting tossed. She said the umpire was very close to tossing me out if I yelled one more insult. As we gathered up our stuff and I put on my coat, she said in a low voice, "You were right. That call in 1968 was BS!" We both laughed heartily and walked out together.

•••

17 A Tribute to a Historic Home Run

This message was written to Willie Mays's personal assistant, Rene. I got a nice reply back from Rene, who assured me she would read this to Willie. Because his eighty-fifth birthday was days away, I'd sent Willie a box of Snickers bars, his favorite. Rene confirmed the Snickers had arrived early and that my idol had already hidden them away in his bedroom! It gave me tremendous happiness to repay Willie in a small way for all the thrills he has provided me, both in his playing days and even now. I was also delighted that he'd hidden my small gift to enjoy all by himself!

I wanted to recognize and honor Willie for what he accomplished fifty years ago tonight! He hit his 512th home run to surpass another Giants legend, Mel Ott, and set the record for the National League. My brother, father, and I were there that May 4th night in 1966.

Every year my father's employer, American Airlines, had a few group outings to the Giants games. They tried to include a few Dodgers games on these group outings. It seemed that every year during the 1960s, the Giants and Dodgers fought a close bitter battle for the NL pennant. We didn't have great seats. But we were still in the lower deck behind third base. I can still see that ball sail over the right field fence like it happened yesterday.

It was the first historic home run that I witnessed firsthand. It was a huge thrill for all of my family. But it was especially thrilling for me. I will never forget my late father turning to me and saying, "Chris! Your man did it for you tonight!" Indeed, it felt like Willie knew his biggest fan, a thirteen-year-old from Fremont, was in attendance. Isn't it special what we can believe in our innocent youth? It is hard to believe that special moment when Willie lined that ball over the right field fence was fifty years ago!

I know Willie has heard these stories untold times over the years. But I'd really appreciate it if you could read this to him. He made one twelve-year-old boy ecstatic that night. For some reason, even though I was a kid, every time I saw Willie play, I realized that I was witnessing something very special. He thrilled me so many times over the years—he was the best *ever*! I know Willie played hard day in and day out, sometimes to exhaustion, for the fans as well as the Giants.

Please tell him:

Thank you for all the thrills!

•••

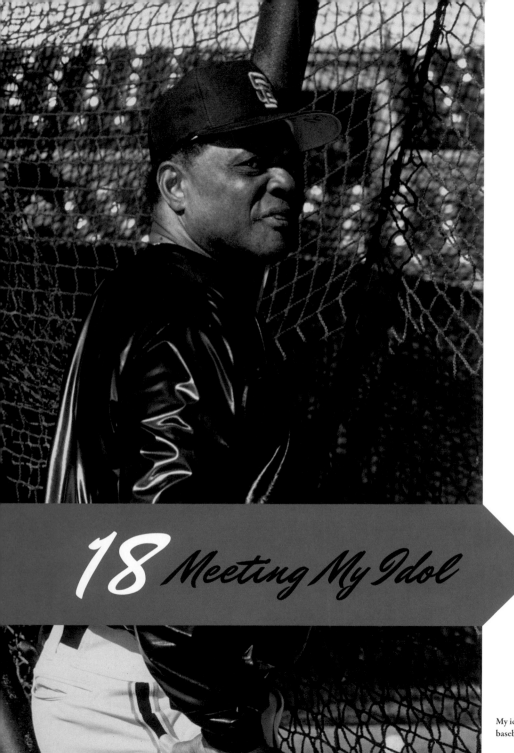

18 Meeting My Idol

My idol, Willie Mays . . . the best
baseball player of all time!

In 2000, my wife and I took our English
friends, Julian and Lizette Hodgson, to the
second game at the new Pacific Bell Park in
San Francisco. It was their first baseball game.
The Giants were playing the Dodgers, and they
only got to see five innings before the game was
postponed due to rain. This was enough time
for me to explain baseball to Julian, and he
became a huge Giants fan in England. By the
way, Julian is a world-class chess grandmaster
and has won the British Chess Championship
four times! He was an extremely quick study.
This was an e-mail I sent to him in late 2014,
after the Giants had won their third World
Series in five years. We were concerned that
they may not sign Pablo Sandoval.

Jules,
I'm with you, along with millions of Giants fans—
they have to keep Panda! He is at his best in the
World Series when the pressure is the greatest. But
I'm afraid he will get some astronomical offers in the
next week that the Giants will not match.

Here's a story about the Panda and my
childhood idol that I think you and Lizette will
both enjoy. Pablo debuted in 2008 with the Giants,
while I was still able to attend the games. During one
late-August game that year, my dear friends Bob and

Audrey, who are part of the ownership group of the Giants, called me. It turned out that the greatest baseball player in history, Willie Mays, also my biggest childhood idol, was thinking of buying a condo in our building. Bob invited me to go up to Willie's suite to talk to him about it!

Jules, I was totally speechless. I was already being mildly affected by the as yet undiagnosed ALS. But my speech was only slightly affected. I was going to meet the biggest idol of my life, sports or otherwise!

When he found out where I was going, my longtime ticket partner, Don O'Leary, insisted on going along with me. So, on wobbly legs, I hurried up to that level of the ballpark with Don. I worried that I wouldn't be able to speak, as I was as nervous as a teenage girl on her first date!

When we got there, Willie stood up, shook our hands with a firm handshake that belied his age of seventy-seven, and invited us to sit down. Words cannot do justice to the surreal feeling that I had. I was really sitting there talking to Willie Mays, who truly is a baseball god! Jules, it would be like you chatting with David Beckham or whoever your biggest childhood sports idol was.

As I talked about the condos to my idol, Panda, who had just been on the team for a week or so, stepped up to the plate. Willie told me that this kid was going to be a great hitter and that he'd given Panda some hitting advice before the game

that night. So what did Pablo do? He promptly hit the next pitch over halfway to the big replica glove we have in left field for his first career home run! Willie, Don, and I shared a laugh over that.

We chatted with Willie for a half an hour. I told him a story of how when I was twelve, I had gotten an autographed ball from him while he sat out the second game of a doubleheader in the bullpen at Candlestick Park. He got a laugh when I told him I used that ball to play catch, being extra careful to make sure my friends were careful to not throw it away and get it dirty. Well, you can guess what happened eventually. That precious souvenir from my idol . . . got ruined! Willie said exactly what I expected him to say when I finished describing how I'd used that ball. He said, "Well, man, that's what a baseball is for—playing!"

When we were about to leave, he asked his assistant, the lovely Rene, to get him a few baseballs. I turned to talk to my friends Bob and Audrey, who had called to invite me up, and thanked them. When I turned back around, Willie handed Don and me an autographed baseball! Willie said, "Now don't play catch with that one!" Don laughed, but I just stared at the precious memento I was holding. Again, I was struck speechless. I finally stammered out a big "I won't, Willie! Thank you!" Then I shook his hand and left.

This next part of the story is almost as amazing as meeting my hero. It also says everything about

how intuitive women are and how well they get to know their husbands. Lizzy had stayed home that night from the game. As I walked across the street to go home, I shoved the precious autographed ball deep into my jacket.

When I walked in, Lizzy was standing in the kitchen. I said with a big smile, "You will *never* guess what happened to me tonight at the game!" I don't know if it was the look in my eyes or how I said it but Lizzy, without batting an eye, said, "You met Willie Mays." For the second time that night I was speechless—a first in my loquacious life! I finally said, "Someone told you." "No, it was that look like you were ten years old that told me," she said. I then pulled out the treasured autographed baseball and showed her. I'm looking at that baseball, my most treasured memento, on my desk as I write this.

Now it's almost two years later, when I was really getting disabled with this horrendous disease. I was sitting down to start a tournament chess game with my opponent. I was so disabled by then my opponents had to travel to my home to play, as I could not drive. As we were adjusting the pieces to start the game, my mobile phone rang and I answered. It was my friend Bob, who immediately said, "Chris, I've got someone here who wants to talk to you."

Next, I heard Willie Mays's distinctive high-pitched voice saying, "Chris, I heard you're battling a terrible disease, and I wanted to call you to say I'm with you in your struggle. Keep fighting." I immediately teared up and my opponent, who was a friend, asked, "What's wrong, Chris?"

I waited until the conversation was over—during which Willie encouraged me to be strong in my fight—then told my opponent, "That was Willie Mays!" His eyes got big, and he said, "No way!" I convinced him it was, and we delayed the game fifteen minutes so I could regain my composure.

I've used that phone call numerous times during the last four years as inspiration to get me through some difficult negative milestones as I've become more disabled. I don't know if Willie Mays fully realizes how a phone call from him can have such a powerful effect on someone like me. Perhaps he does, and that's why he does so much charity work! He's not only a superstar in baseball, he's a bigger superstar as a person! I picked the right man to idolize and plaster my bedroom walls with his pictures when I was so young!

•••

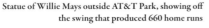

Statue of Willie Mays outside AT&T Park, showing off the swing that produced 660 home runs

19

Hilarious Baseball Story

This was an e-mail written to my ex-Giants buddies Mike Krukow and Richie Aurilia. Liz and I met Kruk when Don O'Leary and I won a Giants Community Fund auction held by the players' wives in 2002. The prize was joining Kruk and Kuip for three innings during a broadcast. It was a thrill to meet both Duane Kuiper and Mike Krukow, two of the best broadcasters in baseball! We met Richie and his lovely wife, Raquel, a year before when we kept running into them at our favorite Italian restaurant, Trattoria Contadina, in North Beach. We later became neighbors with the Aurilias when we moved into the same building. These two are truly some of the most classy and affable of the ex-Giants!

Here's a hilarious story that I read many years ago. I thought a couple of old ballplayers like you guys would appreciate it.

It supposedly was told by Lefty Gomez back in the 1930s. The story takes place in Recreation Park where the San Francisco Seals played before Seals Stadium. By the way, the hospital where I was born in the Mission District was directly across the street from the former site of Recreation Park. Both the hospital and the ballpark are gone now. Here is the story as supposedly told to Babe Ruth:

The main characters in this story are Harry Child and Fred Haney who played for the Los Angeles Angels in the Pacific Coast League. Child was a pitcher who had a glass eye. To hold a runner on second base Child had to contort and turn all the way towards second. Haney was an infielder, who was playing third base the day this story takes place.

Child had a very brief MLB career. He pitched in five games for the 1930 Washington Senators. Haney on the other hand, had a very long 65-year distinguished career in baseball. After a seven year MLB career, in which he batted .275, he was a coach, broadcaster, manager, and general manager. His crowning achievement was managing the Milwaukee Braves to two pennants, including a World Championship in 1957. I remember him as the original Los Angeles Angels General Manager in 1961.

On to the story: The glass-eyed Child was pitching in Recreation Park against the San Francisco Seals, probably in 1929. In the early innings his glass eye popped out. He called time and on his knees frantically started searching the dirt on the mound for his eye. Haney came running over from third and asked what was wrong. Child told him his glass eye had popped out and he couldn't find it. Haney told

him to just go to the locker room and get his spare. Child went to retrieve his spare glass eye and the game resumed.

In the late innings Child spotted his wayward glass eye in the dirt. He it picked out of the dirt and, holding it, called time. Haney ran over from third again and asked what was up now. His teammate said he'd found his lost eye and asked what should he do now with his third eye.

"Stick it up your ass so the guy on second can't get a big lead towards third!" Haney said with a straight face!

Allegedly when Babe Ruth heard this from Lefty Gomez he said, "Goddamn I can't top that one!"

●●●

20 A Few Short Ones

Masanori "Mashi" Murakami,
the first Japanese player in major
league baseball

The short stories in this chapter were originally three separate brief e-mails to family and friends.

Baseball is replete with great humorous stories. Here are a few short stories that I enjoyed. I think you will too!

1. Clogged Base Paths to Stop Thievery

In Herman Franks's first year as Giants manager in 1965, the Giants, like always were battling the Dodgers for the pennant. The base stealer extraordinaire was Maury Wills, who stole ninety-six bases that year. He was a huge part of the Dodgers' offense.

So Herman came up with this idea. In a close game with two out and bases empty, if the pitcher came up, Herman had him walked. Why was this? So that Wills could not lead off the next inning, and if he did get on base, the pitcher on second would clog the base paths and neutralize Maury's speed game. Brilliant!

Herman got away with this a few times until Dodgers' manager Walter Alston finally caught on to what he was doing. In a game late in the season, Franks tried this ploy and could not stifle a laugh as Alston ordered his pitcher to strike out by waving at three balls. LOL!

2. "Mashi"

Another story I found funny was about Masanori Murakami, the left-handed pitcher who was the first Japanese player in MLB and played for the Giants in 1965. He got his one and only start and wanted to bow to the umpire as he took the mound, as was the custom in Japan. Mashi did not speak a word of English.

So his Giants' teammates coached him, and this is what happened as he took the mound. Mashi turned and bowed to home plate ump Chris Pelekoudas and said, "Herro, you haili plick! How you rike to piss up a lope!" Pelekoudas, my favorite umpire back then because he was also *Greek*, could only bow back and smile!

3. Origin of the Gopher Ball

Over the long histry of baseball there have been many colorful characters. But it would be hard to find a more colorful, witty character than Northern California Hall of Famer Vernon "Lefty" Gomez. Gomez was selected to seven straight All Star games in the hitting friendly 1930s and won five World Series with the New York Yankees. Here's an example of what endeared Lefty to all baseball fans for decades.

The old baseball term for a home run is a "gopher ball." It turns out that Lefty Gomez started that in the early 1930s when a reporter asked him if he had a specialty pitch. Lefty replied, "I do have a specialty pitch . . . I call it a go-fer. I throw it and watch it go-fer a double, go-fer a triple, or if I throw a really good one, it go-fer a home run!"

•••

A young Mike Murphy, the venerable clubhouse manager for the Giants, with Vernon Louis "Lefty" Gomez

Despite this not being a baseball story, I would like to pay homage to boxing great Muhammad Ali, who passed away in 2016. Here's my tribute to The Champ.

We truly lost a great one on Friday night with the death of Muhammad Ali. He was undoubtedly the greatest boxer of all time. But he was so much more than a boxer. He was an icon of the twentieth century, a hero to those of us who were opposed to the Vietnam War, and a tireless civil rights crusader.

I was just coming of age and becoming aware of politics when he courageously refused induction into the Army in 1967. Nobody doubted that he would've surely gotten a cushy duty in the Army. Given the rising anger over the war, the last thing the US government needed was for Muhammad Ali to get killed in some rice paddy in Southeast Asia! It's a national tragedy that we lost so many brave young Americans in that way. Ali would've surely been promoting the Army by giving exhibitions and such. He cost himself untold millions and risked prison by standing by his principles.

Whereas I would have volunteered to serve in World War Two, I would have also refused induction

21 The Champ

Muhammad Ali sitting in the San Francisco
Giants' clubhouse

if drafted to fight in Vietnam. Two friends of mine had died and another was never the same due to that disgraceful war. Young people today do not realize the excruciating choices young men had to make because of the draft during that time. Muhammad Ali was a role model for many with his courageous example. His principled stand surely influenced millions to protest the war and perhaps end it sooner.

I will leave it to others to pay tribute to Ali for his monumental contributions to civil rights. As a white male, who didn't experience the indignities of racism, I don't feel qualified to comment on that.

Personally, I had two occasions that involved Ali. One was indirectly and the other was a thrill of a lifetime. Let me describe both.

In 1974, I was working in Oakland on my first job in IT. Our offices were on Edgewater Drive, directly across from the Oakland Coliseum complex. There was a very nice older African American man who was a guard in my office building. Every afternoon, heading into the office, I'd chat with him a few minutes. He was a jewel of a man and we discussed many topics.

That October was the famous fight between Ali and George Foreman, who was the current heavyweight champion. The fight was billed by the colorful Ali as the "Rumble in the Jungle" because it was being held in Zaire. Big George was heavily favored because earlier he had absolutely destroyed the only two boxers who had defeated Ali, Joe Frazier and Ken Norton. Not many gave Ali a chance against Foreman's devastating punching power. In many ways, it was identical to how ten years earlier, in 1964, people thought Sonny Liston might kill Cassius Clay, Muhammad Ali's birth name, in their heavyweight title bout.

It turned out that my guard buddy's other job was caretaker of George Foreman's ranch in Livermore. We obviously discussed the upcoming fight of Ali vs. Foreman in Zaire. Naturally, the hot topic was the Rumble in the Jungle. But whereas he thought his employer, Foreman, was going to whip Ali, I thought Ali would win. We often argued good-naturedly over this as the fight approached.

About a month before the big fight, I was working my normal swing shift. My supervisor called me to the phone. It was my guard buddy, asking me to come to the lobby. I said sure and headed the short distance to meet him.

When I came around the corner into the lobby, who was standing there with my guard friend . . . George Foreman! All six feet four inches of him and he had a vicious scowl on his face as I approached the guard desk. Big George looked massive and menacing. "I heard you think Muhammad Ali is going to whip my ass!" he growled, as he raised a huge fist towards me.

I laughed nervously. But when I glanced at my guard friend, he had a straight face. "Well, do you think he's gonna whip my ass?" George asked, as he waved his fist close to my face. My expression changed to disbelief and concern. Could this be serious? Was the heavyweight champion really angry with me?

My change of expression was the cue for both the guard and George to bust out laughing. Big George unclenched his fist and, still laughing, clapped me on the back. Even that damn near knocked me down!

George couldn't believe that I thought Ali would beat him. He asked if I'd seen the way he had totally destroyed Frazier and Norton. I told him I had. He called Ali an old man and was worried for his health after the fight. I came away from the experience more sure than ever that Ali would win. George was clearly overconfident!

Of course, Ali won with his famous rope-a-dope strategy. After Foreman futilely punched himself out, Ali knocked him out and reclaimed the heavyweight title.

Fast forward four years to early 1978. I'd arrived in Las Vegas on a business trip late at night. When I arrived at the baggage claim area to claim my bag, I was stunned to see Muhammad Ali standing at an adjacent carousel! He was alone and must have just arrived because there wasn't a crowd around him.

When he noticed me gawking at him, he smiled in amusement. Recovering from my shock at being so close to one of my idols, I summoned up my courage and said, "Hi, Champ! Are you waiting for luggage?" I was baffled that he would claim his own luggage!

"Yeah, my driver's a little late," he replied.

I knew he had a fight with Leon Spinks in Las Vegas in a few weeks so I asked, "You here for the bout with Spinks?"

"Yep. Gotta train a few weeks here in Vegas," he answered.

"Well, good luck in the fight. I've always been a big fan of yours," I said.

"Thanks! What's your name?"

"Chris."

"Thanks, Chris!" He smiled and stuck his hand out for a handshake.

I quickly gave him a firm handshake. By this time, a few people had noticed him and came over for autographs. While he patiently signed autographs, I told Ali about my meeting George Foreman before the Rumble in the Jungle and how I told him that I thought Ali would beat him.

Ali grinned widely at this and said, "That big chump could punch. But he didn't figure on the rope-a-dope." With that, he laughed. I smiled back.

My bag arrived, and I wished him good luck in the fight again. He answered, "Thanks, Chris!" With a big grin, I walked away from the gathering crowd around him.

What a thrill! Outside of meeting my baseball idol, Willie Mays, thirty years later, meeting Ali was my biggest thrill! He shook my hand! I was on cloud nine for days!

Sadly, a few weeks later it was painful to see the younger Spinks win against The Champ. As I remember it, it was the first Ali fight on live TV. Seven months later, Ali reclaimed his heavyweight title by beating Leon Spinks in the rematch. It was his unprecedented third time capturing the title. He was unquestionably the Greatest Boxer of All Time.

Tragically, he was afflicted with Parkinson's disease in his prime of life. He bravely battled that devastating disease for thirty-two years. I can only hope to battle ALS with as much courage and grace as The Champ.

Good-bye, Champ. Rest in peace!

•••

22 The Milkman's Day Off

I'd like to share a story written for my children, Monica, Lance, and Stephanie, as well as for my grandchildren, Anthony, Sarah, Julia, Sean, and Jason. It appears for the first time in this book. I'd like to dedicate this story to my dear late eldest daughter, Monica, whom we lost tragically way too young two years ago.

I wrote in an earlier story about how our R & R Construction Yankees dominated the inaugural season of the Fremont American Little League in the summer of 1965 (see "First Time Donning the Tools of Ignorance," page 22). That was definitely my most memorable season in baseball. It was the only team I played on that won a championship. This story is one of the most humorous, troubling, and memorable chapters of that magical season when we were champs!

It was relatively late in the season, and our Yankees had something like a 10–1 record. The only team that had any realistic chance to catch us was the Red Sox. We had just defeated the Red Sox and wouldn't be playing them again for two weeks. Now that I've set the scene, let's get into the story.

In 1965, most families in Fremont had their dairy products delivered to them by a milkman. My best friend, Rick Wilson, had a father that made a

decent living by being a milkman. My family had just added a baby brother in March, and we were now eight strong. I was the eldest of six children; four boys and two girls. We went through a lot of milk! Our milkman delivered the dairy twice a week, and one of those days was Saturday.

We'd had the same milkman since we'd moved to Fremont two years before. His name was Bob and his son, Jeff, played for the rival Red Sox as a pitcher. In fact, Bob's employer, Dutch Mill Dairy, sponsored the Red Sox. Bob usually delivered our milk later on Saturdays

It being summer, I usually slept in late. I wouldn't get up until noon most days if we didn't have an early game. Bob usually talked about his son the pitcher whenever he saw me during his delivery. It was usually just good-natured ribbing like, "My son's gonna strike you out three times Thursday," or some other mild taunt like that.

One Saturday about noon, I'd just gotten up as Bob was delivering the milk. I was sitting groggily eating my cereal when Bob came bounding in the kitchen. He didn't just drop the milk off on the steps. He delivered it right into the refrigerator. My mom was sitting at the other end of the table, drinking coffee and reading the paper.

"Well, you beat us again Thursday. But in two weeks, when we play you again, Jeff's gonna pitch. He's gonna strike you out three times and we're gonna finally beat you!" Bob went into his normal mild chiding. Jeff was a good left-handed pitcher, whom I usually feasted on. I didn't even look up from my cereal. I'd heard that too often from Bob. In fact, I had always hit his son very well, as I normally did against all lefties. My mom didn't bother to look up from her paper either.

"And guess what?" Bob added. I shrugged and said, "What." "We've been getting pitching coaching for Jeff. He's really gonna fan your fanny good next time! And I'm gonna take my first Saturday off in years to witness it firsthand!" he added excitedly. My reaction? I just smiled as I continued chewing my Cheerios.

My mom looked up from her paper with an irritated expression. She didn't like anybody razzing her children. When Bob left, she just said, "Hit a homer, son, so we don't have to hear that crap every time!" I just smiled.

For the next week and a half, Bob kept up his razzing me. Once when he saw me riding my bike, he just held up three fingers in his truck to indicate how many times Jeff was "gonna fan my fanny." I stopped my bike and imitated hitting a long home run! He laughed. I found it all quite amusing. But my mother was letting it get under her skin.

On his final delivery before the game with the Red Sox, Bob was particularly excited talking smack. "It's gonna be so embarrassing for you, Chris! The way Jeff's throwing now, you might not even foul one off!" Mom had had enough. "Oh, yeah! I think Chris is gonna hit a long home run off your son . . . maybe two home runs!" she defended me. Bob shot back, "We'll see Saturday!" With that he held up three fingers and left, smiling.

My mom was steaming though. "How dare he try to psych out a twelve-year-old boy! Chris Loren, you hit a homer off his son to teach him a lesson!" Whenever my mom used my middle name, either

I was in trouble or she wanted to really emphasize something. "I'll try, Mom," was all I could muster.

On Saturday, my mom drove me to the game, which was unusual. She had five others to worry about, and the field was only a half mile away. I usually just rode my bike to the games. My dad was working nights and sleeping days at the time. He too found all this amusing and told my mom not to get so worked up about it. On the way to the game, my mom told me she was staying for an hour or so. That was rare!

When we arrived at the field, Bob was there talking to his son. On seeing me, he held up three fingers and smiled. My mom just made an aggravated guttural sound. She kissed me and said simply, "Do good, son!"

As he warmed up, Jeff did seem to be throwing harder with his new altered motion. I'd been facing him for two years or since we had been in Fremont. I hadn't told my manager or teammates about the razzing from the milkman. I'd let my bat do all my talking.

Finally, the game started. Bob was particularly boisterous in his cheering. We were the visiting team so we batted first. Jeff was also pumped and nervous because his father had put so much pressure on the poor kid. Looking back now, through adult eyes, he was really being unfair to his son to put so much emotion into striking me out and beating us. Of course, then, as an innocent twelve-year-old, I didn't

realize any of that. Jeff walked our feisty All-Star leadoff hitter, Billy Toth.

He got the next batter, and our excellent shortstop, Dave Beebe, was up. As soon as I got on deck, Bob started riding me. I looked at my mom and thought she was gonna go after our milkman! Oh, the silly things parents do while supposedly setting an example for us kids.

Beebe ripped a clean single, and Billy stopped at second. It was time for me to take my hacks. Bob stood up and really let me have it. Even our manager, Mr. Lamont, took note of the loudmouth in the bleachers screaming for his son to "fan his fanny!" I stepped in the batter's box. Jeff's first pitch was way outside, and I took it for ball one.

His next pitch was right down Broadway, and I took a mighty swing at it. It connected solidly right on the sweet spot on the bat! It was a vicious line drive back up the middle. Jeff didn't have time to react at all. The ball crashed into his front landing leg with a sickening crack. It ricocheted off his lower right leg and into foul territory down the right field line. It almost reached the first row of the bleachers, where our milkman was standing up, still mercilessly riding me.

Billy and Beebe scored, and I wound up at third. I knew it was a bad injury from the gasps of the crowd. They normally cheered loudly when there was any scoring. Poor Jeff was rolling around on the ground in front of the mound in severe pain. His father was already by his side, leaning over him by the time I pulled up at third base.

After calling time, I ran over to the gathering crowd around Jeff. He was hurt badly! When it was obvious he wasn't going to shake it off, I said I was sorry. His dad exploded at me yelling, "You did that on purpose! How could you do that!" I was speechless and tried to stammer I did not do it on purpose. Both managers defended me, telling Bob of course I didn't do it on purpose! My mom, who had scrambled down from the bleachers and was on the field now, lit into Bob. "Of course my son didn't do it on purpose, stupid! He's not like that!" For a second, I thought my mom, who was raised on a farm in South Dakota, was gonna go after Bob our milkman! She didn't take crap from anyone. The whole scene was crazy!

Thankfully, the concern shifted back to Jeff. When they pulled his uniform up and took off his stirrup sock, I thought I was gonna pass out. There was a bone almost sticking out of his skin. It was broken right above the foot. His dad and another father quickly carried Jeff to the car and then the hospital.

It was the second time a Red Sox player had suffered a serious injury. A few months before, their catcher, Gary Ribera, had his jaw broken when hit by a pitch. Poor kid was still drinking a liquid diet through a straw.

The moment I saw Jeff's broken ankle, I realized we kids were getting big and strong enough to do serious harm on the diamond. Baseball was and always has been a rough sport. I've always laughed when people who never played much baseball claimed it wasn't. It would only take a fastball in the ribs from even a twelve-year-old to disabuse them of the notion that baseball players are soft!

We ended up winning the game, but my mind was on Jeff and his serious injury. I don't remember how I did the rest of the game but it certainly wasn't very memorable. My mother stayed for the entire time.

On the way home, she had calmed down about Bob's ridiculous accusation that I'd somehow broken his son's leg on purpose. She was concerned about Jeff's injury, too. I think she realized that day, as I did, that kids could get seriously hurt playing baseball. From then on, when I went off to a game, she worried about me much more than before.

When Bob the milkman showed up a few days later, he was very apologetic for his behavior. He said Jeff was doing well and not in pain any longer. He suggested that I should stop by their house to visit Jeff. I promised that I would.

When I visited Jeff, I was sad to see he was in a full leg cast. He was in good spirits considering the injury had ruined his summer. He wanted me to sign his cast. I wrote on the white plaster: *Mavo did this! But NOT on purpose! I'm very sorry. Get well soon Jeff!* When I was done signing, he laughed about what I'd written. Then he told me that the other kids were teasing him. We both laughed hysterically at what they were saying: "Mavo broke Jeff Chinn's shin!" Jeff's last name was Chinn. Say it out loud, and it kinda rhymes.

•••

23 Vin Scully — A Baseball Treasure

Hall of Fame broadcasters Vincent Edward "Vin" Scully
(left) and Lonnie Alexander "Lon" Simmons

It's a pleasure to share this e-mail to KNBR 680's Marty Lurie right before Vin Scully ended his sixty-seven years behind the microphone as the voice of the Dodgers. Mr. Scully is undoubtedly the greatest baseball announcer in history. I'll miss his distinctive voice and the way he painted beautiful baseball memories with it.

I loved the conversation about Vin Scully that you and Bruce Jenkins had this morning. I don't go back as far as you do in Brooklyn. But I did my share of listening to Vin Scully at night on a weak crackling signal from KFI in L.A. back in the classic days of the Giants vs. Dodgers rivalry in the 1960s. Here's a remembrance you might enjoy.

As you no doubt recall, the Giants used to play a lot of day baseball at The Stick. The Dodgers always played their games at night, except on Sundays. And year after year during the '60s, my Giants of Mays, Marichal, McCovey, Cepeda, and Perry were fighting those hated Dodgers for the NL pennant. There were very few games on TV back then. So after listening to Russ and Lon during the day on KSFO radio, at night I'd lie on the floor of my parents' living room with my dad's big console stereo above my head to hear the Dodgers' radio broadcast. I'd lie there tossing a baseball over my head and catching it with my trusty well-broken-in Eddie Mathews glove as I listened.

I'd work carefully to tune in Vinny and his partner, Jerry Doggett, on the weak, distant signal from L.A. The signal was filled with static and faded in and out at the most inopportune times. But I could listen! Compared to today, when you can get not only every team's radio broadcast but also the TV broadcast in HiDef, it was crude. But it seemed magical to my twelve-year-old mind in 1965.

My most vivid memory is of the frantic 1965 pennant race with the despised Dodgers, when Willie Mays won his last MVP. Willie had an August for the ages (I think he still holds the NL record for the most HRs in August). The Giants reeled off fourteen straight wins (still an SF Giants record), even after Juan Marichal was suspended for the Roseboro incident, to take a 4½ game lead in mid-September that year. I thought my Giants were in the World Series for sure.

Then the Dodgers, with a popgun offense, started their own incredible streak of unbelievable pitching to steal the pennant once again. In 2010, when the Giants had that incredible late-season September run of pitching excellence that led to the division title, the only team in modern history that had a better run of pitching excellence . . . those 1965 Dodgers! I vividly remember lying there on my parents' living room floor, listening to Vinny call Sandy Koufax spinning his perfecto against the Cubbies during that tense September race. One of my old Giants heroes, Harvey Kuenn, struck out for the last out. It was classic Scully! (Read "Falling in Love with Baseball" on page 18 to see why Harvey was a favorite.)

As the tension built, Vin painted the scene and described the drama as only he can. In the ninth, with Koufax needing only three outs, he even made a point to note the time and date. The recording of this last inning is available online . . . look it up. Nobody called a baseball game better than Vincent Scully.

So, I too marvel each time I watch the Dodgers on the MLB TV package and hear ol' Vinny still doing it, as I turn sixty-four this year. It's exactly as you and Bruce Jenkins described it, listening to Vinny now takes me back more than fifty years to my youth. He is a true baseball treasure—and this from a guy who hates everything about Dodger blue! A Giants' tip of the cap to Vin Scully's remarkable sixty-seven-year career behind the microphone.

•••

24 Sequel to Meltdown on the Mound

This remembrance was written exclusively for this book. Please read "Meltdown on the Mound" on page 31 for the start of this saga. If you remember, after my meltdown on the mound the prior season, my manager, whose name has been changed for this story, tried to get me barred from playing Babe Ruth baseball in my final fifteen-year-old season in 1968. Fortunately, he was not successful in getting me banned.

Enough people in the league and Fremont youth baseball knew me and knew I wasn't an axe murderer. They also knew all too well of Luis Silva's bad sportsmanship and questionable fitness to be in a position of authority over young boys. In fact, he himself was almost kicked out of the league because parents had complained about his temper and profanity.

Bob Burks, a former opposing manager from my Little League days, who was now managing a Babe Ruth team with his son on it, was my strongest advocate. He remembered how I had torn up the Fremont American Little League and his team in particular three years earlier. He maneuvered somehow to get me on his team for the upcoming season. I'll never forget his call to me when he said, "Chris, how would you like to play for me and stick it to Luis Silva?" It didn't take a second for me to say yes! That call was in December, a good four months before the season. From that date on, I counted the days until I could exact my revenge against Silva!

A few months later, the schedule was released. My new team was playing Silva's team to open up the season. Mr. Burks called to give me the news and ended with this, "And you're my starting pitcher for that game!" Obviously, I was excited by that news. I started working out really hard and throwing to get myself ready for my personal showdown with Silva and his team. I even spent my spare money going to the only batting cages in Fremont. I was extremely motivated to do well and get my just deserts! Revenge in sports is a very powerful motivator. Every second that I pushed myself in my workouts and grunted with my vicious swings in the batting cage, I remembered how Silva had embarrassed me.

About a month before the opener, my new team had its first practice at Washington High. Mr. Burks was delighted to see what good shape I was in. Halfway through practice, he yelled for me to come in from the outfield, where I was shagging for BP. When I trotted in, he introduced me to a pitching guru whose name slips my mind. The pitching guru had coached some at the professional level! I was pumped with excitement when he said he'd be working with me for the remainder of practice.

After warming up, he had me take a few full exertion throws from the wind up and the stretch. He adjusted my stride length, and I'll never forget what he told me next: I was standing too upright when I gathered my weight on my back push-off leg.

There was a light pole right by the bullpen mound. He told me to start to throw the ball over the light pole but stop right before I threw. Looking at him quizzically, I did as told. When I stopped just before throwing, he pointed at my back leg. It was bent at the knee to get the best angle for throwing over the light pole. He said he wanted me to copy that position of my leg and to push off the mound harder before I threw.

When I tried it, I was amazed at how loudly my startled teammate's catcher's mitt popped! It added at least five feet to my fastball!

After working on my grips and smoothing out my mechanics, he said I was good to go. It turned out I was holding my fastball with the seams in a two-seam grip. He had me hold it across the seams in a four-seam grip. That added another foot to my fastball. I was amazed at how a few simple lessons had improved my velocity so much.

Good coaching makes a huge difference throughout sports. But it's especially critical at the youth level. I wonder how many young athletes miss out because they never get good coaching. It has to be millions!

My new skipper was ecstatic when he saw the results of the pitching guru's coaching. "Wait until Silva and his team get a load of that fastball in a few weeks!" Mr. Burks said, beaming.

Sadly, that was the last time I saw that pitching coach. But he sure helped me in just a half hour of coaching

For the remaining weeks before the big game, I continued my hard workouts, hitting in the cages and honing my new pitching mechanics. At first, with the new motion, my control was way off. I was throwing harder than ever but with no idea where the ball was going. My brother and good buddy Rick, who were catching for me, got tired of chasing my wild pitches. But eventually, I got control of my new mechanics.

One side benefit was that my arm felt great after throwing. It really pays to use your whole body to throw a baseball. By pushing off and using my legs more, I took some stress off my arm. This knowledge really helped me when catching later on in semi-pro baseball. I could understand how to help my pitcher better. Another factor was that I'd finally learned it wasn't healthy for my arm to throw a Wiffle ball for hours every night.

The night before the game, I had a very hard time sleeping. I tossed and turned, picturing how I was gonna dominate and get my revenge on Silva for showing me up the previous year. In my mind, I was gonna pitch a no-hitter and hit four homers! I was ready, lack of sleep notwithstanding.

At the game, I had quite an audience cheering me on. My father drove my brother and me to the game. My best friend Rick, who had played on Silva's team with me last year, was there with his twin sister, whom I had dated, and their father. They all took a seat together in the wooden stands right behind the plate. During the drive, my dad had warned me not to be overconfident and it wasn't the end of the world if we lost. I did what all fifteen-year-old boys do . . . I ignored him!

It was May and an overcast, rather cool day. A fairly strong wind blew from right field towards the left field foul line, as it usually did at Washington High, where we were playing. Mr. Silva was up to his old tricks as I warmed up. Knowing better than to directly razz me, he had a few of his players riding me. One of the needlers was Silva's son, Donnie, whom Silva had called in to replace me on the mound when I had my meltdown the previous year. Donnie's heckling surprised me, though, as I thought we'd gotten along well as teammates. Mr. Burks told me to ignore them and stay focused. It turned out Silva had bent the rules and brought in some good players from outside Fremont. The league investigated him later that season, but they couldn't prove anything. He was without shame and a foul-mouthed jerk, but he wasn't dumb!

They were the home team, so we batted first. I was in my customary cleanup spot, hitting fourth. We had a good team too and it was gonna be a good battle, as both teams wanted to start the season with a win.

They had a hard-throwing lefty on the mound whom I'd faced for years in youth baseball. I hit all lefties well, especially him. Our leadoff hitter was Mr. Burks's son, Corky. He drew a walk, and we had our leadoff hitter aboard. He promptly stole second base. We were off and rolling!

The lefty pitching seemed to be throwing harder than I remembered from last year. He struck out the next two batters. As I strode to the plate I locked eyes with Silva, who was standing on the step of the dugout. He smiled wickedly at me. I should've

known what was coming. I continued staring at him as I took my warm-up swings. Taking two deep breaths, I stepped into the batter's box. The first pitch was a heater right at my head! I hit the dirt as Silva let out a sinister laugh.

My manager stormed out of the dugout, as I dusted myself off. My family and friends behind the plate howled in protest. When I looked to the mound, the pitcher just shrugged his shoulders at me as if signaling that he was just following orders.

It was obvious to everyone in attendance that the beanball had been ordered by Silva. After a heated argument by Mr. Burks, the umpire warned Silva, who couldn't hide his amusement. All the umpires in the league knew the whole sorry tale from last year. They all disliked Silva. They knew he was a hotheaded blowhard.

The argument gave me time to regain my composure. Taking three deep breaths this time, I stepped in again. The next pitch was right down the middle. I rifled it right back up the middle into center field for a single. Corky steamed around third to score. As I ran to first, I shot a dirty gesture to Silva surreptitiously. My cheering section behind the plate erupted in hysterical cheers. It wasn't the home run I'd vividly imagined during my sleepless night, but it felt really good anyway.

Our next batter was the right fielder, who had good speed. He hit a groundball into the hole between third and shortstop. The shortstop had to dive to stop the grounder. He knew there was no play

at first. I chugged for second as fast as my short legs would carry me! The only play was at second base. Silva's son, Donnie, the second baseman, was already on the bag with his back turned to me, waiting for the throw. My job was to break up the play and try to take his legs out.

The hurried throw from the shortstop arrived at the same moment as I did. I slid into Donnie, taking his legs out. I have to give him credit; he held on to the ball as he fell on top of me. The base umpire bellowed, "Out!"

Next thing I knew, Donnie shoved me as he jumped to his feet. It had been a totally clean play on my part. If I'd wanted to, I could have easily cut him up with my metal spikes while knocking the little bugger halfway into left field. But I didn't play baseball like that. I jumped up and pushed him hard. He then called me something best left unwritten in this book. I got him in a headlock and squeezed as he thrashed about futilely! "You little *bleeping bleep*! If you don't wanna play the infield, maybe your dad oughta have you pitch!" I said. It was, of course, a reference to how his father had embarrassed me the previous year by putting Donnie, who never pitched, in to relieve me.

Right then, the beefy first baseman got a hold of me and pulled me off Donnie. We squared off to fight. Both teams were by now out on the field, exchanging pleasantries, of course.

The base umpire was a big guy who, together with the home plate umpire, restored order quickly without any punches thrown. Silva was screaming that it was a dirty slide, and I should be tossed out of the game. I realized, in horror, that the umpires might throw both of us out. My revenge game would end with my getting thrown out of my first game! The base umpire, who was right on top of the play, disagreed and said Donnie had pushed me first. After both managers had their say, nobody got tossed. Whew!

Back in the dugout, Mr. Burks took me aside. He placed both hands on my shoulders to get my undivided attention and said to calm down. But it was useless, though well-intentioned, advice. The revenge factor already had me psyched out of my mind before the game. The donnybrook (Sorry, dear reader, for using that cheap pun!) at second base now had me a slobbering, crazy fifteen-year-old, heading to the mound, although somehow I convinced Mr. Burks that I was calmed down and ready to focus.

My heart was still racing as I took the mound and during my warm-up throws. I turned my back to the plate and took numerous deep breaths. No use! All I did was nearly hyperventilate. Silva was in his customary third base coach's box to my right. He began needling me right away, saying things like, "C'mon, Donnie, this guy's got nothing!" Donnie Silva, who had a miniscule strike zone, stepped into the batter's box.

The adrenaline coursing through my veins was making me nauseous as I unleashed my first pitch almost to the backstop. My gaze went to my cheering section right behind the plate. My dad was yelling to settle down. None of my next three pitches were close, and Donnie jogged to first, clapping his hands. Silva gloated, "What'd I tell you! This guy has got nothing! He can't hit the broadside of a barn!" Mr. Burks yelled at Silva to knock it off, to which he just laughed.

The next batter hit a little nubber up the third base line. After almost colliding with my catcher, I promptly heaved it over the first baseman's head down the right field line. The batter coasted into second, as Donnie raced to third. This wasn't at all like I'd dreamed it would be!

Up next was a left-handed batter. He hit a screaming line drive that my first baseman speared. Mr. Burks visited the mound to tell me to calm down and that I was overthrowing. After he returned to the dugout, I thought I was gripping the ball too hard.

I decided to go back to my old upright motion, figuring at least I could control my pitches better while giving up some velocity. One of Silva's imported ringers was digging in the left-handed batter's box. He was the huge first baseman who had pulled me off Donnie. He even looked scary with his scowl as he dug in. My old motion seemed to work as I got two quick strikes, as the frightening batter nearly came out of his shoes with vicious swings. The adrenaline had subsided, and I thought I could get out of the inning with our 1–0 lead intact. Wrong!

My old motion had me striding shorter than the motion I'd learned from the pitching guru. This meant my left foot landed about six inches short of where the new motion had me landing. There was a deep divot where my foot had been landing with the new delivery. With the count 0–2, I intended to throw my next pitch low and outside to have this aggressive hacker chase it. But on the pitch, my foot landed halfway in and out of the divot I'd previously made. It threw off my balance, and my intended low outside pitch ended up right down the middle! My heart sank as he took a mighty hack and connected with a thunderous crack!

There was no need to look where the ball was headed. It was crushed! It sailed well over the right field fence for a tape measure three-run homer. They now led 3–1. As the hitter rounded third, I heard Silva say to him, "What'd I tell you! You're gonna kill this bum!" Rage boiled up in me and, for a moment, I thought of charging Silva to teach the old cuss a lesson. Somehow, I resisted the urge.

I won't bore you with the play-by-play of the rest of the inning. I will tell you it was embarrassing. By the time I got out of the inning, we trailed 5–1. I fired my glove into the wall with a loud yell when I finally got back to the dugout. Mr. Burks came to me a few minutes later, when I'd regained some sanity, and told me he was bringing in a new pitcher the next inning. I understood completely. I felt awful about my pitiful display on the mound. I'd let the situation and anger take over. After my frustration subsided a bit, I realized what a difference it made playing for a good man like Mr. Burks. If I'd been playing for Silva, he'd surely have embarrassed me out there.

As I sat in the dugout and calmed down, I had a baseball epiphany! At that moment I finally realized that baseball was not to be played with gung ho emotions, like football. No, baseball required cool nerves and focus. Only then could your natural motor skills blossom fully. You need great motor skills to excel at baseball. It doesn't lend itself to blind emotion. I laugh when I hear fans today say that baseball players need to play with more emotion. In baseball, you need to relax and focus, not be some maniac spitting fire. After my talk with Mr. Burks, I promised myself I'd play the rest of the game without so much emotion and use focus instead.

The bottom of our lineup scratched out a run. As I trotted out to left field for the bottom of the second, we trailed 5–2. I ignored Silva's attempts at heckling me, as I passed him on my way to left field. I was determined to ignore his taunts and play the remainder of this game with focus to let my motor skills work to their fullest.

Our new pitcher, whom I'd traded positions with, was indeed focused and he struck out the side in the home second. I came up again in the top of the third inning, with two on and one out. This time I was totally in the moment and not reliving my embarrassment from a year earlier. The lefty on the hill was laboring and had thrown a lot of pitches already in the inning. He threw me two outside fastballs that weren't close. With the count 2–0, he threw another fastball. This one was fat!

I can't begin to describe the feeling of utter euphoria when I swung with everything I had and connected solidly. Nowadays they call it "squaring it up." We didn't have that jargon back then. Let's just say I hit the snot out of it. My little cheering section behind the plate erupted in wild cheers the instant the ball left my bat. Everybody in the ballpark knew where the ball was headed.

I trotted around first base as the ball settled well over the left field fence. It was as far as the opposing first baseman had hit his to right in the first. This time I ignored Silva and there weren't any nasty gestures from me. "Damn it! I told you to keep it away from him!" Silva moaned as I passed. It was tied now, 5 all. Game on! I reminded myself to stay focused and in the moment as I crossed home plate.

It remained tied into the home fifth. Usually, when I wasn't catching or pitching, I played first base or right field because of my arm. Mr. Burks didn't want to move everybody around so he had me playing left field. The ball came off the bat and moved differently than I was used to in right field. So far while playing left field, I'd only had one routine fly ball hit to me. With a runner on second, a right-handed batter hit a wicked line drive my way. It was coming right at me off the bat. But then I froze in terror. It was knuckling!

Anybody who's played the outfield will understand my terror. When a ball is hit just right, it doesn't spin. That makes the ball dance crazily and unpredictably like a knuckleball does. But a ball hit hard enough to make it knuckle is much more violent in its crazy trajectory. I tried to stay with it, but it was just about to sail over my head. I jumped as high as I could and luckily snagged it in the web of my glove. Silva, never one to let an opportunity to whine pass by, let out a loud, groaning, "That was horseshoes!"

In the sixth inning, I came to bat again with a runner on second and one out. There was a sidearm throwing right-hander on the mound by now. Worse, I had never faced him like I had the lefty from our Little League days. He threw at a very unorthodox angle, especially for a right-handed batter like me. He was probably one of Silva's illegal imports. I had real trouble keeping my front side in there. Every pitch looked like it was going to hit my hip. I weakly struck out. The next batter hit a routine groundball to third, and the third baseman threw it away! The runner scored from second, and we led 6–5!

We held them scoreless in the bottom of the sixth by turning a pretty double play to end the inning. In Babe Ruth baseball, a game is only seven innings. One more inning, and we'd beat 'em! Silva looked miserable as he trudged to the dugout after the double play. I couldn't resist a loud, derisive laugh as I passed him.

When they came up in the last of the seventh, it was still 6–5, good guys! Donnie led off by roping a single into right field. Our pitcher, who had relieved me in the second inning, was tiring. Mr. Burks brought in a new hard-throwing right-hander. He struck out the next batter, but Donnie stole second base on the first pitch. He had speed and now was in scoring position with the potential tying run. It was nervous time.

My nervousness increased when our pitcher walked the third place hitter. Up stepped their cleanup hitter to the plate. He was the big, scary left-handed-batting first baseman who had hit the mammoth three-run homer off me in the first inning. Mr. Burks called time and came to the mound. When he was done giving our pitcher the standard baseball pep talk, he patted him on the butt and, on his way back to the dugout, motioned for all us outfielders to back up. I backed up almost to the warning track in front of the fence. He wasn't gonna hit over my head unless he hit it out!

On the first pitch, he hit a little pop-up right over third base. With a huge adrenaline rush, I sprang into a dash to track it down. I simply had to catch it! As I looked up towards the rapidly falling ball, I heard Silva yell to his son, "Go! Go! He'll never catch it!"

I was desperate as I frantically chased the pop-up. The shortstop couldn't get to it because he had been playing over towards second base for a possible game-ending double play. The third baseman was also frantically chasing it, running with his back to the plate. It seemed as if everything was happening in slow motion as I made my desperate

dash for the ball. Silva was still yelling "Go! Go! Go!" to both runners. If I didn't catch this pop-up and it bounced away from me, both runners could score and we'd lose. I just had to catch it. The ball was twisting towards the foul line because of the wind and how the batter had sliced it to his opposite field. I adjusted my route towards the ball.

The third baseman and shortstop were closing in on it, too. It appeared I could just get there in time, so I started yelling, "I GOT IT! I GOT IT!" as loudly as I could on a dead run. The shortstop backed off, as he heard me calling for it. But the third baseman kept running with his back to the plate. I could get there, but I'd have to dive if I was going to catch it.

At the last possible instant I thought of playing it safe, pulling up and playing it on the bounce. That would at least keep the game tied because the runner couldn't score from first. *No, I could catch it!* I dove and reached my glove out backhanded as far as I could. Inches from the ground, the ball landed in my glove. I'd caught it, miraculously!

While I skidded to a stop on the grass on my belly, the third baseman tripped over me. I held on to the ball tightly as he let out a groan as he hit the deck, too. What had taken mere seconds had seemed to me like minutes.

I jumped up, holding the ball high over my head to show the umpires I had indeed caught it. The bases umpire, who had run halfway into the outfield, bellowed "Out!" I looked at Silva, who was close by in the third base coach's box.

For once, the loudmouthed-miscreant was momentarily silent. He was in shock that I'd caught it. Our eyes met for a delicious moment that's forever etched into my memory. His expression of utter shock and misery was, oh, so sweet for me as I just smiled at him.

Donnie had already crossed home plate, and his dad started frantically yelling, "Get back! Get back!" The desperate shriek of Silva's to get back is also a sweet memory for me still, after almost fifty years! Mr. Burks was yelling too, for me to get the ball to second base for the game-ending double play. Donnie started racing back towards second base. I jogged towards second, too.

Our second baseman was already standing on the bag, smiling broadly and waiting for my throw. Donnie gave up his hopeless running as he rounded third. Not wanting to risk a throw even this close, I continued my joyous jog. When I reached the bag, I didn't just touch it normally. Instead, I jumped and stomped triumphantly on it.

Game over! And sadly, dear reader, book over!

•••